BEYOND SINGLENESS

BEYOND SINGLENESS

HOW TO MAKE BETTER RELATIONSHIPS

HELENA WILKINSON

RoperPenberthy Publishing Ltd
Horsham, England

Published by RoperPenberthy Publishing Ltd
PO Box 545, Horsham, England RH12 4QW
www.roperpenberthy.co.uk

ISBN 978-1-903905-29-6

Cover design by Angie Moyler

Typeset by Avocet Typeset, Chilton, Aylesbury, Bucks
Printed in the United Kingdom by Haynes, Sparkford, England

CONTENTS

Introduction

In the early 1990s I was commissioned to write a book on singleness – the original manuscript for *Beyond Singleness*. Five authors prior to me had had their manuscripts turned down; mine was accepted. On that basis one might have thought that I was an advocate for single people and had a calling to speak on the subject; not so! I simply had personal experience, had talked with many people for whom being single was proving to be a challenge and could craft a manuscript which addressed some of the issues.

Putting *Beyond Singleness* together exposed an attitude difference that sometimes exists in the church between married and single people and opened my own eyes to the different battles that single people face. I carried out my research well and at the time of writing the book I felt I had all the material I needed. After it was published I received many letters. One letter said, 'If you will excuse me saying so, I think that you are much too young to write a book on singleness'. I struggled to see the writer's point - I had just about made it to thirty and had spoken to a whole spectrum of single people prior to compiling the manuscript. Now I am in my early forties, still single and still desiring marriage, I know exactly what the writer of the letter was saying; struggling with singleness when there is plenty of time on your hands is one thing, but a whole new perspective is added when one is getting older and the biological clock is ticking.

Rather than being a book for singles on how to handle being single, my brief in being commissioned to write

Beyond Singleness was that it should be a book for the whole Church, exposing an often ignored issue. Some churches are good at addressing singleness, others are not. Singles have questions which remain unasked and statements which remain unspoken, mostly because they fear what people will say or know that others won't listen. *Beyond Singleness* is not a book of answers: it comes from one who is in the midst of a process and is always learning; it is rather a book to stimulate communication. We owe it to others to share what we learn.

Although I put this manuscript together over ten years ago and it was first published in 1994, I have chosen not to alter the contents or title. However, re-examining the book I did wonder why I called it *Beyond Singleness*. The reason at the time was that it was part of a series of books I was writing with a 'Beyond' theme. However it did make me think when someone recently said, 'Surely beyond singleness is marriage?' For a moment I felt she had a point and then I thought a little more – beyond singleness there could be marriage but more importantly beyond the struggle of singleness there is acceptance. I hope that as you read this book it will challenge and encourage you and that you will find something within its content that takes you beyond where you currently are!

Helena Wilkinson, Swansea 2006

PART 1
STUCK IN THE MUD

1 | *Feelings and fears*

> I close the door at night and the walls encompass me. The air is filled with emptiness and I long to be held, but no one's there. As I lie down it is as though my body is being crushed, crushed by my own thoughts, aspirations, failed dreams. I feel as if I would rather do anything than be on my own. There is life bursting inside me, bursting to love and be loved, but nowhere for it to be channelled. I am too tired to get up and look, to go out and meet. Tonight will be another night of me, my feelings and my fears.

Why does singleness feel so agonising at times? Is it because society has dictated that partnership is the norm? Or is it because we are made for companionship and crave our 'other half', in whom we find deep satisfaction at a physical and emotional level? Perhaps it is that we feel of value, both in our own eyes and in the eyes of other people, when loved, and being seen to be loved, by a partner. We all need to know that we are loved, and the longing to be loved is probably the greatest factor behind the 'sting' of singleness. Not having a partner to whom a commitment has been made leaves the single person feeling on his/her own, and being on your own, when you haven't learned how to handle it, feels oppressive and at times frightening. It inevitably creates a void from which it seems there is no escape other than marriage.

In thinking about singleness I have become aware of five main feelings with which people struggle: loneliness, fear, pain, anger, worthlessness.

Loneliness

Loneliness is like cancer of the soul, eating away, leaving devastation which, at first, is not visible to the outside world. Many people are haunted by emptiness, but fail to equate this with loneliness. Perhaps we need to ask ourselves questions which run far deeper than the obvious 'Am I lonely because I am on my own?' Do I:

- find it difficult to trust others?
- frequently worry that others may not accept me?
- feel guilty most of the time?
- often feel inferior to others?
- find criticism difficult to handle?
- constantly seek acceptance by others?
- live in fear of rejection?
- worry too much about my friendships?
- tend to overvalue and rely too heavily on one particular person?
- have a tendency to daydream?
- feel that I lack the social skills that others have?
- struggle to feel that I belong?
- find it difficult to tell others how I feel when they have hurt me?
- often feel emotionally empty?
- consider that I have felt lonely all my life?

Maybe some of these statements are not ones with which we would naturally associate loneliness but they help us to distinguish between what I believe are two types of loneliness: *loneliness,* as when we want to spend time with people and no-one is around; and the *state of loneliness,* which has not so much to do with circumstances as it has to do with connections.

How do you put into words the inner anguish? Loneliness is a word which underestimates the intensity and agony of the *state of loneliness*. It is like being trapped in a deep pit which has tunnels leading to dead ends. All around is space and each echo of one's own voice acts as a crushing reminder of the hollowness and the desolation. Its poison takes hold through lack of bonding, not feeling accepted and not belonging. Circumstances perpetuate the feeling but the root goes deep into the personality of the individual and his/her past. The *state of loneliness* leaves a person feeling 'on the edge', aching, longing, empty and hungry.

The hardest part is that often the person doesn't understand why he/she feels this way. Not being married may become the explanation of the pain but I believe that loneliness to this extent runs so deep, and is so entrenched in the person, that marriage will not bring about the much sought-for solution. What is needed is an untwisting of the tangled roots which have left the person like a gnarled tree. Simply changing the outside will not sort out what lies beneath the surface.

The doctors from the Minirth-Meier Clinic define loneliness as: '... a state of feeling that one is not accepted or does not belong. It implies varying degrees of emotional pain, an empty feeling, a yearning to be with someone, a restlessness.'[1] From their study of the Bible and their experience as psychiatrists they have found there are five general causes of loneliness:

- isolation from God
- our changing society
- rejection of others
- being rejected by others
- neglect in childhood

At the foundation of loneliness, whether the loneliness is through lack of peace within ourselves or as a result of circumstances which accentuate feelings, there is the fact that we need love, acceptance and affirmation from others. Loneliness arises out of the desire to have someone close to us; someone who is interested in our life; someone who cares about what we do a are; someone who is committed to and believe

Loneliness can have such an ugly grip that, w feeling cannot be expressed and is not being under by other people, it leads to depression. Behav patterns may develop as a means of trying to cope: workaholism, compulsive eating, promiscuity, drug and alcohol addictions, tranquilliser dependency, self-harm, anxiety, over-spiritualising, shyness, withdrawal, seeking attention, etc. The inability of a person to communicate how he / she truly feels, perhaps because of the fear of not being properly heard, leads to having to act out the pain in these various forms. The final escape for some people is suicide, or attempted suicide, as a declaration of the agony they feel. Figures show that suicide rates for single men are three times higher than for married men, and for single women twice as high as for married women.[2] Most people who look to suicide feel alone – too alone to ask for help.

Fortunately for the majority of people their loneliness never brings them to the point of considering such a drastic option as attempted suicide; it just sits like a cloud ready to engulf or cast a shadow over the person. It hurts to feel that there is no one around with whom to share thoughts and feelings, especially when walking into an empty house at the end of a working day. For some the morning can be difficult, waking up alone; for others the night is the dreaded time, when minutes seem to extend to hours. When living alone, loneliness can result in what appears to be a personality change: the front door is closed and a different life is led from the one exposed to the working world during the day. There is no one to point out that patterns are moving beyond the coping level to the destructive, and the person can live a quiet life of desperation. Fear and pain become exaggerated and psychological problems can develop through lack of perspective on life and interest in the outside world.

As one watches friends of the same age find someone special and disappear into the land of couples, courting and marriage, it is easy to feel more and more alone, even isolated. It is not just a matter of *being* unattached, but *feeling* unattached. For those who have been married and have known companionship, the sudden change through death or divorce can throw one into what is terrifyingly unfamiliar territory. June, who had had a good marriage and been widowed, found that one of the hardest aspects of being single and adjusting to her new life was 'dreading another lonely twenty-four hours'.

For people living on their own, having to do everything oneself can create feelings of deep loneliness, especially if the person finds it hard to ask for help or has not been able to form the kind of friendships which lead to mutual supportive care. I look back on my early days of living alone and struggling with doing jobs single-handed. 'It's all right for those who've got a man', I screamed inside as I battled with heavy jobs around the house. Now, whether it is through having more supportive friends or greater skills in coercing people to help (or both), I find that instead of coping alone I tackle the more troublesome things with others. Other people ask the same of me. One friend who finds it difficult to do her course study on her own sometimes asks if she can sit in my room and study whilst I tap away on the computer. Her ability to ask results in not being alone in her work, which shows that much of our experience of 'struggling by ourselves' is perhaps due to a difficulty in allowing others into our world.

Being in an environment of high expectations, having to act as if nothing is wrong or being controlled by others can also lead to intense loneliness. These experiences are fairly common in pressurised jobs or some types of churches where members feel the pain of not being allowed to be 'real'. The person begins to live a split life: separating his/her true feelings from those which are 'allowed' to be shown to the outside world. Negative feelings tend to be dealt with in the privacy of one's own company. Contrary to many people's belief that success brings happiness, loneliness can increase with success, compounding the false image that 'everything's OK'. The successful person is somehow expected to 'have it all together'. Lois Frankel, a counsellor devoted to women in crisis in transition, said: 'As my private practice of psychotherapy began to grow, I became aware that many of my clients were talented, attractive, competent, bright ... and depressed ... a common thread that emerged was that in order to be successful, these women felt they had to be free from feelings and emotions.'[3]

The person who is in the *state of loneliness* can find it hard to understand how others can be content when alone or in solitude, and has difficulty in seeing being alone as a potentially creative time. There is the fear that 'if I feel so terribly desolate *with* others, being on my own for life might be unbearable'. But if we are not careful we move into self-pity, self-absorption and jealousy, which are one-way tickets to chronic loneliness. It might be true that we all get lonely, but we also choose whether or not we stay lonely. We either tackle the problem or give in to it. Most people take the second option because it doesn't involve as much risk or stepping out in faith, and it means we can avoid having to look at the way in which we relate to others.

How can we overcome our loneliness? Firstly, we need to realise that we have to help ourselves; others are not going to come and rescue us. Secondly, we need to understand where our loneliness comes from; to realise that the cause of our loneliness could be far greater than simply being single. It is said that 'loneliness has its beginnings in childhood between the ages of one and three. It is a root condition of life and it is during these post-embryonic years that we first begin to experience doubt as to our self-worth.'[4]

Around my early to mid-twenties I suffered acute loneliness. 'Why?' I asked myself. I had written a best-seller; my name and picture had appeared in papers and magazines all over the country; I had appeared on radio and television; I was in a lively church with a young people's group; I had friends. The answer was that I did not know how to relate to people and I still had unfinished business from childhood. I lived in a state of needing to be rescued, except when I was busy rescuing others. My past hurts held me prisoner, and prevented me from making connections with people.

Now I less frequently taste the bitterness of loneliness, mainly because I have improved relational skills and have some deep, meaningful and fun friendships. I know acceptance and care and I realise also that I have choices. I have discovered that it is up to me to choose with whom I associate or form a bond. I don't have to be controlled and obligated, but rather can be fulfilled and confident in making decisions and forming my own opinions. I have learnt (and am learning) to know and to trust myself. All these, and many other discoveries, bring a freedom which is far from the trap of a self-perpetuating loneliness.

The key to freedom from the *state of loneliness* is 'connectedness'. Connection begins to happen when you *know* acceptance and love from God and others; allow yourself to *feel* that acceptance and love; you create ways to *bring about* acceptance and love for yourself. It also occurs when you take an interest in people and life; let go of being a perfectionist; let go of false guilt; find release from the effects of emotional damage in childhood. Loneliness lessens when you feel understood, but to feel understood you have to communicate. Yet feeling understood is not sufficient: the release comes in living out your faith, in being able to be yourself and enjoy life.

Much as we enjoy life we have to accept that there will remain moments in our lives when we will still be touched by a level of loneliness, and this is normal. At first glimpse, the sight of loneliness is bleak, but within the bleakness is the seed of magnificent blossom. In rejecting the bleakness we may be rejecting the potential for new growth.

Fear

So many singles live with the feeling that 'one day' they will marry, and as the years go by an increasing fear arises: 'What if' "one day" is *never*?' The thought of what might not happen starts to become the fear of reality. This fear is so often kept locked away because of other people's judgement of the single person not trusting enough. 'Perfect love casts out fear' is quoted at the struggling individual, with the hidden, and sometimes not so hidden, message of 'Your faith is not sufficient' or 'You haven't handed your singleness over to God'. Whilst this may be partly true the hurting individual is now not only trying to handle his/her fears but suffocating under a mound of guilt.

Perhaps one of the greatest fears is the fear of rejection. For most people the fear is based on experience. When you have been rejected once, there is a little voice inside which says 'When is it going to happen again?' Rejection results from the denial of love.

> When one is loved, he is approved and accepted; when one is rejected he is disapproved and refused. The hurts of rejection are synonymous with refusal, denial, turndown, rebuff, repellence, cold shoulder, slighting, shunning, spurning, ignoring, neglecting, avoiding and disapproving.
>
> Each of us requires love. Love is necessary for the development of a healthy 'self-love'. Love is to us what sunshine and water are to a growing flower … Rejection causes a wound to 'self' … Once the wound of rejection is introduced into a person's life, two

> parallel problems begin to emerge: fear of rejection and self-rejection ... One who is rejected, who is put down by others, is prone to put himself down.[5]

The fear of rejection grows not only out of broken relationships as an adult but also past hurts as a child: abuse, neglect, control, bullying, peer rejection, etc. Each time, as an adult, we receive rejection; if we have not dealt with earlier rejections it intensifies the experience. Unhealed rejections can so easily lead to bitterness, withdrawal and self-focus. Moving into these reactions often causes further rejection: 'Life becomes a merry-go-round of hurt, reaction, rejection – and it is anything but merry.'[6]

Dwelling on what we fear can cause the fear itself to become a reality. Most damaging is the self-rejection which follows rejection from other people. The fear of rejection only adds to the experience of loneliness, but until we let go of self-rejection we will never escape the grip of the *state of loneliness*. When we have tried to get close and have been rebuffed it makes it harder or takes more courage the next time. We need to hold on to the truth that 'The person who rejects you is making a statement about himself or herself – not about you.'[7]

Besides the fear of rejection or of not finding a partner, other fears which single people have talked about have been:

- the unknown
- meeting someone when you are too old to have children
- asking God to reveal his plan for your life, in case it doesn't include marriage
- being ill and having to cope alone
- losing one's parents and being totally alone in the world
- choosing the wrong partner

- marrying someone and then finding 'Mr / s Right' elsewhere
- being hurt again and again in relationships
- falling in love when the other person wants to keep the friendship platonic
- becoming or being regarded as an 'oddity'
- not being able to get work, especially where there is responsibility for children
- losing children the day they become independent and leave home
- losing friends once they get engaged and married
- not making new friends following the disappearance of old ones
- being alone
- being misunderstood
- becoming selfish, or of self-pity taking over
- getting close to others, or letting others know the 'real' me
- being left out, or feeling a misfit
- leaving things 'too late'
- being 'trapped' in a relationship which is not working
- failure, or not being good enough
- what other people might think
- making irrational decisions when alone for too long
- being latched onto by strange people

Each set of fears is unique to the individual. The only common factor is that people need to be, and feel, *understood,* not condemned for their fears. As they are understood they can be helped to sort out their fears, become objective and begin to let go in such a way that they can admit to how they feel but not let the feeling dominate or control their lives.

Pain

Emotional pain can pierce and tear and leave a person feeling raw. Single people may carry deep hurts for many reasons. For the divorced person there may have been rejection, alienation, emotional cruelty or bitterness leading up to the divorce. Intense pain may linger and yet there is the necessity to carry on with everyday life in order to survive financially – the combination is not easy to handle. Margaret's husband left her for another woman: 'My friends did help in practical and in loving ways but the devastation I experienced took four years to get over and it was so difficult, even though I knew God was with me'. When in pain you may frequently try to talk to someone but the words become watered down the minute you open your mouth; or you become aware that the one who is 'listening' belittles what you are saying, perhaps through lack of knowing how it really feels.

The single parent can sometimes feel hurt when seeing a mother, father and children as a whole unit. Being separated can be a very painful place too: where the individual can feel that he/she is neither totally single, in the sense that there is not a complete break; and yet not married, in the sense that the marriage is not up and running. Other people's attitudes towards the separated person ('not able to stay married and not having the courage to make the break') only intensify the feelings. For many singles who have never married it hurts to see people happily married with families when, inside, that is their greatest desire. It looks so cosy and the single person feels so cold. Going to church can feel a little like playing 'happy families' when, painfully, one is the 'solo single'.

The pain of singleness runs far deeper than not being, and yet desiring to be, married. I have a friend in her late twenties who struggles to relate to men. She has never 'dated' so has never been in a position to relate couple-to-couple, unlike some of us who have had several such experiences. The pain which she feels is agonising. This and other types of hurt seep into our sexuality and the essence of *us* as people, and can feel like a rejection of these very things. The mid to late twenties is quite a significant time as one watches the big '3' '0' looming nearer – the time by which many often expect to be married. Wendy, who is twenty-six, wrote to me: 'It seems as though I am hungry and yet not allowed to be hungry, and I watch other people satisfy their hunger. It hurts feeling so available as a woman and yet no one seems to want to marry me'.

Closely linked to the fear of rejection is the pain of betrayal: in relationships, friendships and churches. Dr Dan Montgomery says that 'Betrayal is like having an axe laid to the tender roots of our being.'[8] He points out that Webster's dictionary defines betrayal in the following ways: 'to break faith with; to deceive; to lead astray; to seduce and then abandon; or to fail to meet the hope of'. He talks about four vital qualities of the healthy personality – Love, Assertion, Weakness and Strength – and how these polarities need to be fulfilled and in balance. 'In the process of recovery, we rediscover and reintegrate whichever polarities have been lost. *Love* provides the emotional glue of specialness and intimacy. *Assertion* serves the purpose of maintaining fair play and a balance of power. *Weakness* adds vulnerability and the awareness of our needs. *Strength* preserves autonomy and self-esteem.'[9]

We want	**We get**	**We feel**	**We become**
Love	Betrayed	Fearful	Anxious
Assertion	Intimidated	Helpless	Manipulative
Weakness	Exploited	Distrusting	Avoidant
Strength	Humiliated	Insecure	Artificial

Beneath the façade of what we become lies pain. The cause of the pain may be different for each person. An experience which seems futile to one person can feel like agony to another. I don't believe that people's pain can be compared. The cry of the human heart is that someone else would enter into our pain with us and be there for us. Some of the most precious moments I have had in my life have been when I have been hurting intensely and someone has been there for me. If a person can do this, how much more can God?

I don't know if in the church we are very good at 'being with' a person when he/she is hurting. So often the expectation for God to 'zap' the pain or for the person to summon up the faith to 'let go' of the pain robs the carer of true empathy and robs the person who is hurting from feeling understood. When I read the Bible and look at some of the great Christian men and women, I see people who wrestled with, and grew through, such pain. They did not run for a panacea. They found freedom in their faith.

At times, as a single, life can hurt so much. Feelings can range from vague sadness to utter despair. If you don't understand why you feel a certain way it intensifies the hopelessness you feel. When you understand why, it releases you to look at what options you have.

Anger

Often behind pain lurks unexpressed or buried anger. If the single person who longs to be married is honest he/she will find that at some stage in the journey anger is very present. Why do singles become angry? Because:

- there is a sense of being cheated out of what is most desired
- seeing others get married and have a family emphasises what we lack
- it is as though life is moving on for everyone else and we are 'frozen in time'
- life does not feel fair
- there are desires which aren't being fulfilled
- other people are always making the assumption that

you are married or in a relationship, as though singleness isn't a state to be considered.

Anger is a very real emotion and should not be ignored. However, within our own lives we need to sort out the difference between what is anger at a seemingly unjust situation or difficult circumstance, and what is anger as the foundation for bitterness and resentment. Holding on to anger destroys us spiritually and emotionally.

How do we know if we are angry?

Anger can only be extracted when recognised for what it is – pent up energy. The following physical changes indicate the stress caused by anger, hurt, grief and disgust.

- Are your muscles tense around the eyes?
- Is your jaw set and are your teeth clenched?
- Are your throat muscles tight?
- Has your pulse rate accelerated?
- Are your hands doubled up into fists or even slightly closed?
- Do you feel any tension across the upper and lower back?
- Is breathing becoming more rapid?
- Is your stomach tense, knotted up, quivering or upset?
- Do your leg muscles feel taut?

We see two patterns here – a speeding up of the rhythm of our body (circulation and breathing) and a tightening up of the muscles. The body is making preparations to fight or take flight.[10]

Since anger is a secondary emotion – usually fuelled by and following on from pain, loss or disappointment – it needs to be dealt with, not stored up. If it isn't dealt with as each issue arises it can so easily come out at another, perhaps inappropriate time, attached to a different situation or directed at another person. Depending on the nature of the anger it needs to be acknowledged, expressed and confessed.

Anger which is pushed down can result in depression. So often people deny not only the fact that they are angry but the fact that they are depressed too. Soon these people are merely living in existence, having deadened all negative feelings and consequently being unable to feel love and joy. They are left feeling a vague greyness and wondering what is wrong. Often there is little thought as to why the person feels like this. Depression goes undetected partly because people don't understand how it shows itself. 'Depression is manifested through four key areas: our feelings, our thoughts, our behaviours and our physical functioning.'[11]

If we do not deal with anger but direct it at ourselves it can also turn into guilt. We need to get in touch with the pain behind the anger. As a counselling friend from Ohio says: 'The next time you feel angry, pause for a moment, breathe into your anger, and ask yourself, "What is threatening or hurting me?"' Staying with the pain is not what will bring freedom. Forgiveness brings true freedom.

Worthlessness

Sometimes negative feelings towards the single state result in feelings of worthlessness or low self-esteem. On the other hand, if the person already has low self-esteem, he/she may assume that this is the reason for still being single. Whether the feelings of worthlessness are the *cause* or the *consequence* of being single, such feelings and beliefs will not be helping the single person to get the most out of life. I think it is fair to assume that the majority of people who find it hard to cope with their singleness also struggle with negative feelings towards themselves. We need to like ourselves in order to like life – whether that is single or married life.

We also need to be confident in ourselves to withstand insensitive comments from other people. In one church of which I was a member I had started dating a guy when a married man made the comment to him: 'Helena's extremely attractive, but she's nearly thirty and not married ...' In other words, 'what's wrong with her?' (I wonder what he'd say now that I'm in my early forties and still not married ... definitely something wrong with her!) At the time, my ability to be confident in my own beliefs about myself was not high and I began to believe that this man (who hardly knew me) had a more accurate assessment of me than I did. 'Perhaps there is something wrong with me,' I thought. Yet inside I knew that the reason I was not married was partly through working long hours and not mixing, partly because I was not ready to get married, and partly because God has a plan for my life and I now realise that marriage was not on His agenda at the time.

We need to know, like and respect ourselves because, unless we do, each negative comment which comes will knock us flat. It's not that we shouldn't consider other people's points of view, and at times they may be right, but we should have enough regard for ourselves to be able to assess comments and attitudes accurately and make our own judgments. We need to ask ourselves, 'Is external or internal validation more important?'

Talking to a number of single people I have listened to feelings which reveal extraordinary inner pain. One man in his late forties described feeling like 'an outsider' because he is single; others have talked about feeling 'ostracised', 'unwanted', 'like a leper', 'different', 'a failure', 'out of place', 'ignored' and 'humiliated'. Other feelings which are reported by singles include anxiety, guilt, disappointment, disillusionment, lostness, frustration, desolation, bleakness, blackness, emptiness, hopelessness, shame, envy and confusion. In an attempt to help a single person, and to help myself, I would want to take an honest look at those feelings and sort out which ones are truly connected with singleness, and which ones actually stem from another aspect of life but are accentuated by being single.

For many single people the greatest struggle is the thought that one has to try to cope with these emotions, and the battle with worthlessness, alone. 'At least the married person has a partner to talk to,' singles lament. My whole belief about this concept has changed over the years; there are many married people who do not have a partner to talk to because their partner does not understand or cannot communicate at the same level. There is also the fact that in some situations emotions can be more fully understood by someone of the same sex. I have some very good friends with whom I can share deeply and since being able to do this my perception that I need to be married in order to know care and understanding has altered.

What unhappily single people need is not necessarily a marriage partner at this point but a committed, available friend who can empathise and have the patience to listen. The difficulty within our culture is that so many people do not want to admit to feelings of loneliness, fear, pain, anger and worthlessness. People walk around wearing their 'I'm OK' masks, which leaves others feeling, 'I'm the only one who seems to be struggling with this "singleness thing".' If only we could all talk and share the ways in which we have struggled, and what we have found helpful, we might find that singleness isn't so bad after all!

2 | *Sex and Sexuality*

When researching this book I asked a group of singles to write down their fears and apprehensions related to singleness. One man in his late twenties said that he feared 'dying before the opportunity to have sex'! Talking specifically about sexuality, another man in his early thirties said: 'I feel as if there is no outlet to express my sexuality. It has broken a number of friendships and caused me considerable pain. It seems that my sexuality is the one aspect of me that everyone rejects and it has become a millstone around my neck.' Ninety per cent of the Christian singles I spoke to felt that the Church's teaching on sexuality (and how to handle the frustrations of not being able to be in a sexual relationship) is not adequate.

Unsatisfied sexual desires can become the focus of anger towards being single. With each relationship the single person has to abide by the 'so far and no further' rule (amongst other 'rules') which has stemmed out of the Church's correct teaching of no sex before marriage. To the single who has not been encouraged to explore the *whole* concept of sexuality, the 'rules' seem only to lead to the frustrating feeling that fulfilment is *just* out of reach. The single person, like anyone, is constantly confronted with sex by the media. To the abstaining single the media emphasis on sexual fulfilment is like a sweetshop window to the child who is being punished by deprivation – the goodies are so close at hand, but you can't have them!

Besides the 'rules' there are the clichés which many

church leaders and married people use as they discuss sexual matters with a single person. Kathy Keay brings a little humour into this delicate subject in her 'diary to God':

> I find the old, well-worn clichés on the subject increasingly unconvincing. Like the other night, for example. There was this panel on Christianity, Sex and the Morality of Personal Relationships. When it came to the question on Sex before Marriage, which for some of us could be rephrased, Sex before Death (i.e. if at all), Mr Upright had this to say: 'The only legitimate context for sexual activity is marriage; that is why a man leaves his father's household, cleaves to his wife and they become one flesh'. Just like that, I thought, to say nothing about the woman of course! But what about those who have left their father's household for ten, fifteen, twenty years, whose fathers are dead and they still ain't found anyone to cleave to? There was no answer to that. A single woman in her mid-thirties replied, 'It seems to me all very well, Mr Upright, to uphold the ideal of marriage, and I notice you speak yourself as a married man, but vast numbers of us have been left feeling that our sexuality has been outlawed.'[1]

Denial of sexual feelings

Being a Christian was never meant to involve the denial of sexual feelings, and yet some of the 'advice' or 'attitudes' which come through members of the church can lead a single person to believe that he/she is not supposed to have such feelings, and that the day the person stands before God in Holy Matrimony these feelings are miraculously awakened! 'Christian books abound on sexual technique for married Christians, but little exists on sexuality for the unmarried which is not insultingly simplistic. After all, people reason, what is there to write about abstaining? Sex is seen as fulfilment; virginity as a vacuum.'[2] Do we really believe that people are unspiritual if they talk about sexuality and sex when they are not married?

In speaking of sexuality we have to consider that normal single sexuality will include physical aspects such as menstruation, tender breasts and spontaneous erection. There can be sexual dreams as well as a general sexual interest in others in response to emotional or visual stimuli. Women may notice that it is normal to experience increased sexual awareness at certain stages in the ovulation cycle, and for both sexes there will be the longing for loving emotional and physical relationships. Such experiences are not a breach of the standards of Christianity. These are not lustful, although they can become so.

Very few people have no interest in sexual matters. This interest can be as healthy as any other interest or activity, but any function if not handled carefully may get out of hand. Therefore, we need to guard against slipping into unhealthy thought patterns and practices. Our sexuality has often been defined too narrowly and legalistically, i.e. 'No sexual contact outside marriage' – end of comment on sexuality. This very negative attitude imposes on single people a heavy burden of denying or suppressing any sexual feelings or thoughts. For some people this has resulted in emotional or psychological problems.

There is a myth which seems to exist that says you are not an adult until you've had sex. A similar myth, often created within the church through the inference from many married people, is that singles are not fully mature. It not only hurts but it is ludicrous when the single person is treated as ignorant, asexual or still a child because he/she 'shouldn't know that kind of thing'. So many times I have observed group conversations where it seems 'OK' for a young married woman, maybe only twenty, to mention sex (or the opposite sex's anatomy) but it is completely 'out' for a single woman, in say her forties, to speak about these matters. What about the single person who is a nurse or doctor or counsellor and knows much? What about the single person who has been sexually abused, molested or raped? Is that person completely ignorant? What about the single person who had several sexual relationships before even becoming a Christian or has had a sexual relationship since becoming a Christian and perhaps has mixed feelings of satisfaction and guilt? Then there is the mass media, which leaves very little to the imagination! In fact, singles who 'know nothing' are undoubtedly rarer than those who are aware.

Be warned!

We need to be informed, but be warned of how reading sexually-stimulating material does stimulate! 'Reading sexually-stimulating material while trying to remain celibate is like reading a *Gourmet* magazine while sticking to a diet. We only have so much resistance and once our minds are won over to a concept, it is not long before our bodies follow. We must not assume that purity means naïveté.'[3]

The Church's teaching of no sex outside marriage is emphasised not only because it is one of the 'commandments of Christianity' but because sex is intended to be an expression of *total* giving of self and comes within the bounds of commitment to each other in marriage before God. Sadly, through the years, sex has become self-centred – a way of meeting one's own needs – and has been distorted and purported to be the ultimate in individual happiness. However, 'Experience shows that sex outside the context of a loving, committed relationship increases feelings of low value, of rejection and of being discarded.'[4]

The Office of Population Censuses and Surveys also

revealed that couples who co-habit before marriage are more likely to divorce than those who do not.

Despite these facts, the decision for the single person to remain celibate and keep sex for marriage (should marriage ever be a part of his/her life) is not easy for most people. Some singles find it difficult even knowing *why* they should remain celibate. Norman Wright speaks of five positive reasons:

1. There will be no guilt over having disobeyed God.
2. There will be no fears of conceiving a child and having to decide what to do next.
3. There will not be the comparing of a future spouse's sexual performance with that of past lovers.
4. The self-control learned by waiting for marriage will be valuable.
5. The pleasure of sexual satisfaction shared only with each other will bring excitement into your life and marriage.[5]

People who are free to engage in the sexual act with their husband/wife, or those who have learned to cope with the desires, can easily belittle the extent of sexual frustration a single person can feel. Singles who hold to Christian principles are under huge pressure. Part of the pressure is that many non-Christians consider life without sex as quite abnormal – to say nothing of the person who abstains! Celibacy immediately conjures up an image of someone who is joyless, passionless, immature, prudish and even uncaring! Personal worth is at times aligned to sexual achievement, leaving many singles who choose celibacy with the feeling that they have failed.

Choosing to be celibate is certainly misunderstood by many people but everyone is misunderstood at some stage. Are we going to throw away something precious just so that we can be seen to be 'OK' in the eyes of those who hold different views? In the end, does it matter what others think? We need to learn to be confident in what we believe, and feel good for believing it rather than being apologetic. It is important to know that if you choose celibacy it is still possible to love someone deeply, to express affection and to feel the wonderful rewards in doing so.

Sacrifice of holding back

What is required is a 'holding back', which is essentially a *sacrifice*. Julia Duin, in her book *Sex and the Single Christian*, points out: 'Granted that sex represents the most vital and most intense sensual experience of which the body is capable and that sexual surrender involves subordination to the other, who are we to do it so casually? We are laying bare our souls as well as our bodies ... How little our culture understands or emphasises sacrifice,'[6] It has also been said that 'God intended sex to be a bonding experience as powerful as the bonding that takes place between a mother and a child at birth. If you constantly tear away at that bond, pretty soon you lose your ability to bond ...'[7]

Although anyone can succumb to sexual temptation people 'who have been robbed of deserved love are especially vulnerable to the temptations of sexual sins. The love hungry are deceived into thinking that their love need can be met by gratifying their sexual appetites in illicit ways.'[8] Overcome by pressure or desire, some Christians will have found themselves unable to 'hold back' and so will have slept with someone, and as a result may be plagued by guilt, often too ashamed to talk to anyone. When they do talk they are often on the receiving end of attitudes which result in further hurt; treated as though sex before marriage is the most corrupt of sins. I don't believe we should 'grade' sins, but sexual sin is noted in the Bible as being different because it is a sin against the body and the body is the temple of the Holy Spirit (see 1 Corinthians 6:18–19). I have encountered several Christians who, as a result of giving in to sexual temptations, have been treated as outcasts by their churches. Yet Scripture teaches that *If we confess our sins, he is faithful and just and will forgive us our sins and purify us from all unrighteousness* (1 John 1:9 NIV).

A fuller understanding of sexuality

I have already mentioned that the Church often defines sexuality too narrowly. As Christian singles we need to get in touch with our *whole sexuality*, knowing that a small part of it (genital activity) is inappropriate at this particular time. What is our whole sexuality? It is difficult to define, but it has to do with much more than sexual feelings towards another person. It is something which infiltrates every area of our life and is expressed in all that we do or say. It has to do with our identity as males and females, involving things like: caring, giving, sensual pleasure (through all the senses), creativity, receiving and giving affection, using our imagination to enrich our own lives and the lives of other people. We express our sexuality in many ways including our choice of colour, clothes, style and décor – everything!

The more in touch we are with our sexuality the greater the sense we have of knowing ourselves as individuals, and the greater our sense of choice. For example, in the area of clothes we would move from wearing something simply because it is the fashion, or what we were brought up to wear, to wearing something which expresses our personality.

'Single people are not sexless beings, but men and women with the same sexual energy as married people. The Church has often denied single people a positive approach to embracing and expressing our sexuality … God places limits on our sexual behaviour, but not on the expression of sexuality. The problem is that the world has limited our understanding of sexuality to sexual intercourse ...'[9] The Bible doesn't have much *explicit* teaching on this subject for those seeking specific moral guidance. Singles will need to search out for themselves what is applicable to them from broad biblical statements.

Although the Bible sets boundaries on sexual behaviour outside marriage, the Church often interprets this as a denial of sexuality. No wonder there are pent-up feelings and frustrated individuals! We *need* expression of our sexuality just as we need to breathe, eat, sleep and communicate. Once we have separated out sexuality from the *act of sex* we can begin to look at different but acceptable ways of expressing sexuality. For women this might include:

- use of make-up, clothing, hairstyle, jewellery, perfume
- finding the style of dress that best suits you and you feel enhances your femininity or your identity
- use of décor in the home
- use of the more feminine character qualities, e.g. caring, gentleness, creativity
- bringing the feminine touch into mixed-sex planning (e.g. use of flowers for events, etc)
- a meaningful friendship with affirmation from the opposite sex as a means of enhancing and complementing our sexuality
- acceptance of the body and a healthy love for it expressed in the enjoyment of food, exercise, posture and bodily care
- physical (but non-sexual) contact with both sexes

For men this might include: sport, friendship, style and dress, music, the need to create or build something. We are all a mix of feminine and masculine and women may need encouragement to achieve, take responsibility, etc.

and men may need a safe place in which to feel vulnerable.

Maybe some people reading this will feel angry: 'I don't care about those things; they are no substitute for sex!' True! But the more we understand and give expression to our femininity or masculinity, allow our needs to be met in legitimate ways, and learn to ask when in need, the less we will be frustrated about the lack of genital sex.

Struggles

The Christian single has been taught that he/she must stand out as different from non-Christian peers. The stress on being different and the lack of adequate positive and practical teaching on sexuality together produce a lethal result: confusion, frustration, pain, guilt and shame. Asserting one's sexuality without being immoral can seem like a losing battle. This is partly because we are sexual beings and so need to express our sexuality; and partly because people struggle to differentiate between desire and lust, between sex and sexuality. 'Lust ... may be described as a perversion of desire ... When desire says "I just have what I want, whatever it may cost to others or however it may affect my relationship with God", then it becomes lust.'[10]

When you become a Christian your moral stand may perhaps be quite different from what it was before conversion. People who have known sexual involvement or who have been caught in certain habitual patterns, such as the use of pornography, can really struggle. High levels of sexual frustration can sometimes cause people to regret being a Christian. Those who have been married or have encountered sexual intimacy can miss the reassurance and relaxation which is experienced in a relationship with another. Or, to put it bluntly, one can simply miss sex and orgasm! Masturbation becomes one way to handle these feelings. Depending on the teaching which the single person has received on masturbation, he/she may be left feeling confused, guilty or dissatisfied. And of course, so often, there is no one to talk to because in many churches there is taboo about these kinds of subjects.

One question many singles ask is whether masturbation is allowable. Dr Angelo Grazioli, a sex therapist in South Africa, says that many Christian singles come to his clinic concerning masturbation because all they have heard in their church were meaningless clichés:

> Masturbation was clearly understood in biblical times. The Mesopotamians thought it was a terrible thing; the Egyptians thought it was OK for people of high class but not for the working class. The Greeks considered it acceptable. Yet there is not a word on it in Scripture. There are lists of sexual sins but masturbation never comes up, which is significant in itself ... However, there are many people for whom masturbation is destructive because they have abused their sexuality through the use of it.
>
> Masturbation is a self-centred practice; it denies the very communication and communion for which sexuality was designed. As a functional, one-off, non-addictive means of release I believe it's OK, but if it becomes a compulsion then it is a problem. It is similar to alcohol. Wine isn't sin in a bottle but for an alcoholic even a glass with a meal is wrong ... As with any compulsive behaviour the addict has to understand what he is getting out of it, what lies he is telling himself, and what goals are being reached by this compulsion. One has to nip the real problem in the bud, which, almost invariably, in a young man who is a compulsive masturbator, is not a physical or even a sexual problem. The compulsive masturbator doesn't know how to express his masculinity or interact heterosexually in a healthy, non-genital way. I

> wouldn't get this person to memorise Scripture verses or take cold showers, but rather to understand how he can express his masculinity in a God-given way.[11]

Fantasising becomes another way of coping. For some this means simply fantasising about having a certain partner, whilst for others there can be slavery to fantasy which is sexually explicit in nature. Whilst vague day-dreaming about dating a certain person seems relatively harmless, sexually explicit fantasies are dangerous and can be counter-productive. They often draw a person away from being able to relate to others.

People who, as children, were shy, or did not learn social skills of interaction with others, may feel embarrassed about their sexuality. Some people who may never have a boyfriend/girlfriend are left asking, 'How do you ever move into the real world of relationships? How do you rid yourself of the apprehensions about dating or the fears of sex?'

The need to be held

Many Christian singles struggle with the longing to be loved by someone else: not just to be loved in a general sense, but to be held in a very particular way. This may have a sexual, or in many cases an emotional, driving force behind it. The longing for emotional needs to be met can cause a person to be more involved sexually in a relationship than he/she believes is right. There are complications in the relationship which 'goes too far' and further complications when it breaks up. A break-up which has not involved a sexual relationship is painful enough, but it is more painful where a person has given of self in this way. One can feel 'used' or 'exposed' or filled with self-contempt for 'stretching the boundaries' or entering into a total union.

More difficult than saying 'no' to sex is knowing how far is 'too far'. This is a difficult question, and it is impossible to draw a clear line between where one sort of kissing and touching ends and another begins for every couple, but a guiding principle is to ask oneself: 'What effect is this type of interaction having on me (in terms of character, spirituality and integrity) and upon the person I am spiritually with?'

Apart from natural sexual desire, perhaps we have to look at the underlying emotional reasons for the temptation to get more sexually involved. These will be different for each person. Quite a few years ago, after reading one of Michel Quoist's prayers, I found myself looking at and writing about my own desire to 'stretch the boundaries' in a relationship.

I want to love, Lord,
I need to love.
All my being is desire;
My heart,
My body,
Yearn in the night towards an unknown one to love.
My arms thrash about and I can seize on no object for my love.
I am alone and want to be two.
I speak, and no one is there to listen.
I live, and no one is there to share my life.
Why be so rich and have no one to enrich?
Where does this love come from?
Where is it going?
I want to love, Lord,
I need to love.
Here this evening, Lord, is all my love, unused.[12]

When I first started going out with one particular boyfriend I felt we could trust ourselves, yet within only a couple of months desires were growing and I felt as if I was going to lose the battle. What would another three months bring? It seemed that whilst socialising with other people our relationship was one of growth and enjoyment, but when alone it was filled with desires which were difficult to control and compromised satisfaction. I felt confused. Being physically close gave me a sense of security, yet afterwards I felt guilty and would quietly purge the pain in tears.

Although I believed that I had come to terms with being single, looking back I can see that lying beneath my behaviour was the fact that I had never actually come to terms with one aspect of it: that not getting married might result in no physical warmth. I felt a great deal of internal conflict: guilt, fear, disappointment, sadness and, strangely, very mixed feelings of love and hate. Hidden even more deeply, as I know now, were anger and anxiety.

My means of discovering what I was searching for was to ask myself: 'What am I hoping to accomplish through my behaviour?' The honest answer was security and love. I remember the bullying I received at boarding school at the age of ten. I was put on 'trial' and in failing to answer questions (which were tricks) I received punishment: sharp compass points were stuck in my back, piercing the delicate skin. Lying huddled underneath my bed I felt isolated and my heart throbbed with pain. Day after day I longed to be loved and held. Words were almost meaningless; what spoke to me of love and what I wanted was *touch*. The need was actually emotional, but when in relationship I assumed it was sexual and hence a relationship which moved towards marriage was the ultimate solution to my need for warmth and security.

God spoke to me very clearly about my behaviour, saying, *For whoever keeps the whole law and yet stumbles at just one point is guilty of breaking all of it* (James 2:10 NIV). I became aware of a particular sin described in New Testament Greek, *parabasis,* which literally means crossing the boundary line. 'The word pictures someone disregarding a "No Trespassing" sign ...'[13] I realised that I could not grow spiritually if I violated God's standards and misused my sexual drive. *Remember the height from which you have fallen! Repent* ... (Revelation 2:5 NIV) ... *return to me and obey my commands* ... (Nehemiah 1:9 NIV) ... *Be faithful, even to the point of death, and I will give you the crown of life* (Revelation 2:10 NIV).

Repentance, meaning a complete change around from that which is self-centred to that which is God-centred, required a profound change in my thinking. Reading a book one day I noticed that the authors pointed out: 'We get two things confused: "I need" and "I want". To change our thinking we also need to "Disconnect the triggers that set off the bomb".'[14] For me this meant dealing with the childhood hurts which were causing me to long for physical contact, whether this was expressed through emotional warmth in a friendship or physical closeness in a relationship.

Church change

A large part of the single person's struggles to come to terms with his/her sexuality has to do with the Church and its teaching. Much of the responsibility for teaching is with married men who have not had long periods of singleness. Lack of experience in this area can lead to a tendency to be legalistic, or to a temptation to be simplistic. Whether the Church means to or not, it has in the past often given a negative view of sexuality, and some of that negativity seems to be reflected today.

> Origen taught that sex was inherently wrong, and designed only for procreation. He had himself castrated. Chrysostom likened women's bodies to beautiful burying places. Jerome banned all married couples from communion if they had had sex the night before. Augustine maintained that sex was the result of original sin. Lombard maintained that the Holy

> Spirit leaves the room when a couple has sex ... Such unbiblical perspectives led to equating celibacy with spirituality and advocating sexless marriage, in direct contradiction of the New Testament (1 Corinthians 7:3–5). By the time the Church's head cleared and it said, 'Really it's not sex we're against but the misuse of sex', no one was listening.[15]

The lack of freedom to talk about such struggles puts people in the position of not understanding their sexuality. People seem to turn to the Church as a point of moral reference and also to receive help when struggling. Emma, who is twenty-nine, told me how her church had caused her great confusion.

> No one encouraged me to see myself as a sexual being. In fact it was quite the opposite – because I was not married I was somehow asexual. It was as though any conversation into which sexuality crept came to an abrupt end when they realised that I, an unmarried woman, was present. Yet inside I *felt* sexual! After a while I became afraid to admit these feelings, even to myself. I pushed the feelings aside and each time they came just labelled myself as 'bad'. But the trouble was that the more I pushed them aside the more obsessed I became. Soon I was fantasising and even beginning to carry out some of my fantasies. It was frightening. Only when I sought the help of a counsellor did I begin to realise that it was the suppression of the feelings and the unnatural lack of expression – the denying a real part of me – which was causing the behaviour patterns. As soon as I got in touch with my sexuality and found acceptable ways of expressing it, which enabled me to feel a 'full' woman, the thoughts and actions, which had been so alien and yet so powerful, went.

I wonder if, in the Church, we are doing the person a favour or causing damage if we set 'rules' but fail to talk about the larger issues. There is a need for more down-to-earth teaching on sexuality, and although the pulpit may not be the place, there should still be opportunity to air thoughts, feelings, longings and fears without judgement. If someone declares something very definite about sexuality, such as 'no sex before marriage', people need to understand *why* and *how to cope*. If you understand why and make a decision, you move from *obligation* to *choice*. Unless this happens we will just go on perpetuating the cycle of suppression and guilt.

Laden with guilt

How many people are walking around unnecessarily laden with guilt for thoughts and actions associated with sexuality – people who feel trapped in a corner with no one to talk to? The advice for handling sexual feelings is often very unhelpful: 'You mustn't act in this way'; 'Take up a hobby'; 'Ask God to take away the feelings'; 'Read Scripture to purify your mind'. Maybe some of these are extreme examples, but the fact is that pushing away or covering up these very real human feelings does not bring about resolve.

Some members of the church use Scripture passages to show the single person how fortunate he/she is still to be single. However, the way in which Scripture is used can be patronising. It is good to be reminded of one's freedom and the benefits of not having a partner or family, but this must be handled sensitively. Possibly the most quoted passage is from 1 Corinthians, where Paul basically says that, in his opinion, it is better to stay single than it is to marry. He goes on to say, *But if they cannot control themselves, they should marry, for it is better to marry than to burn with passion* (7:9 NIV). What is often missed out is that Paul is addressing those people who have a particular partner in mind.

The trouble with using excerpts from the Bible such as this, often taken out of context, to 'speak to a single' is that the one doing the quoting is often not *hearing* the hurt of the single. It leaves the single person thinking 'If only it were so simple – that there was even someone with whom to form a relationship or to marry!' Some people when given passages are left feeling angry, others anxious, and others fearful. It is important to find out first, before giving biblical quotes to someone, whether that person is at a place where he/she can receive them.

It is also important for the single person to be allowed to talk about fears, and this includes fears associated with sexuality. Exposed fears are often not as threatening as those pushed inside and dwelt upon in the middle of the night. In a survey I carried out I unearthed some of the fears singles have. One man in his early thirties said he feared that sex wouldn't be as enjoyable as it is made out to be. One woman in her mid-forties said that she constantly struggles with the desire to have affairs with married men, which feels 'safer' than dating unmarried men because there is no commitment. Several women said they feared that it might not be possible for them to have children. The fear is psychological, rather than being based on a physical reality, but nevertheless it is significant. One of the women, in her late twenties, was asked by her GP to go for a smear test. She had had a few gynaecological problems and the doctor carried out an internal examination. As the doctor talked about and pointed out her ovaries and womb the woman suddenly felt mature, maternal, and womanly. '*My* ovaries!' she repeated to herself. She had only thought of ovaries as being associated with a child-bearing woman, someone who was sexually active. 'I didn't really think about sexual reproductive organs as belonging to me, a single woman! It felt so good!'

Helping ourselves

Although the Church has the potential to help the struggling single person by its recognition that single people are sexual beings and its willingness to talk about these issues, ultimately the single person has to help him/herself. Perhaps most important is the person's ability to accept him/herself as a sexual person. Sexual desire is a part of each person's identity; a part of our God-given human nature.

We need to learn to *live through* sexual longings, not just get rid of them as though they are alien. If you never allow yourself to live through longings or feelings, but always push them away, you may never discover that not only can you survive and cope the next time they come, but also grow as an individual through them. Such longings do not have to dominate the whole of your life, but unless understood and embraced, they may. Just because you *feel* a certain impulse doesn't mean to say that you have to *act it out*. Experiencing sexual desire is not wrong. Following that feeling to the point of breaking the Bible's teaching on what is appropriate is wrong.

Knowing you have choices, and knowing that intimacy is not here today and gone tomorrow, may help to prevent acting in an extreme manner. I relate this principle when helping people with eating disorders. Knowing that chocolate will still be available tomorrow frees the person not to *have* to eat the whole box today! If you ordinarily deny yourself chocolate – you are more likely to binge on it! The same, I believe, applies to our sexuality. The person who shuts down intimacy in all forms to prevent 'going too far' can, when faced with a relationship, feel the urgency to get all he/she is able out of it. Intimacy and sex are appetites in the same way in which hunger is an appetite: the hungrier you are, the more you want to eat! We can satisfy the needs of our sexuality in many different ways. For the person in the midst of the pain and frustration of celibacy it can feel as though genital satisfaction is the *only* satisfaction – and he/she is cruelly denied it.

People cope with unfulfilled longings and desires in different ways. It has been said that our sexual drive is the creative drive. Karina, a divorced woman in her mid-thirties, copes by converting her sexual feelings into creative energy: 'I paint very large acrylic paintings!' Some people believe that we are more sexually frustrated if we are not socially fulfilled, and so have found that increased general relating lessens desires. Each person needs to build up his/her own list of how to handle the more frustrating and difficult times. I think it would be wrong for me to write a specific, graded list of 'how to cope with sexual feelings'. I can only write down some aspects of coping which I and others have found helpful:

- get to know your body clock and which times are the most difficult
- think through coping strategies rather than just waiting for things to happen
- get to know how you, as an individual, handle sexual tension
- be clear in your own mind as to what is 'acceptable'
- recognise your areas of weakness which could lead you into sin
- realise the need for, and work out, how you will achieve self-control
- learn to say 'no', so that you do not allow others to persuade you to do anything against your wishes or beliefs
- avoid situations or TV programmes which can lead to frustration and pain
- find someone you can talk to and pray with
- develop meaningful non-sexual friendships which partially fulfil the longing for closeness

Expressing sexuality

Helping oneself is far more than just discovering a means of handling the frustration. It is about being in touch with your sexuality in a way that brings you alive as a person, but does not compromise Scripture. Single Christians need to learn to enjoy being a man or a woman, and to enjoy the company of the opposite sex without needing to be flirtatious, fearful, guilty or awkward. Sexuality is expressed through the individual's interaction, opinions, feelings, handling of situations, etc. It is far more than biological facts! Julia Duin talks about her method of handling sexual feelings:

> … there are the times when all the hugs, activities and cold showers can't dispel our longings for sex. I've found it's best not to ignore these longings but to perceive the wellsprings of love and tenderness and giving that want to be expressed sexually. So I take certain factors involved in sex, such as being vulnerable and surrendered, and express them in a non-sexual way.[16]

I think the concept of taking the factors involved in sex and finding another way of expressing them is particularly helpful. It takes thought to discover the factors because it means actually looking deeply at what is happening to us emotionally within an experience such as sex.

Equal consideration needs to be given as to how these factors can be sublimated. I used to struggle to accept and express my sexuality. Initially this was very much shown through my rejection of a woman's body when I had anorexia. But later it was more subtle: rather than a rejection of my sexuality, it was a 'being out of touch' with it. Experiences in my earlier years had led to a revulsion and fear in connection with sexuality. I could present myself as feminine in how I dressed, but I was not aware of choice when expressing this aspect of me. Interestingly, as I worked on these issues which had troubled me I became more aware of my femininity, and found myself growing my hair, painting my nails, wanting to express something of myself (which was distinctly feminine) in the décor in my house, etc. I can now distinguish those things as expressions of my femininity and feel good about them. Before I couldn't even feel! When in need of warmth I can ask for a hug; before I found asking too difficult!

Discovering ways of expressing our sexuality is liberating and is vital for the single person who wants to move from frustration to freedom.

3 | LONGINGS AND LOSSES

People long for many things, and as a result of unfulfilled longings they experience loss. In some circumstances the loss is an *actual* loss and in other circumstances it is a *perceived* loss. Either way, a grief or bereavement process, which usually goes unnoticed, can begin. A synonym for the word 'bereave', found in the *Complete Wordfinder*, is the word 'rob'[1] which indicates that the experience encompasses a feeling of something meaningful missing. For the single person who longs for marriage the feeling of 'something missing' is very descriptive – he/she knows exactly what isn't there!

There are countless longings which a person can have in relation to being single. The longing to:

- feel cared for
- be cherished
- be special to someone
- be affirmed
- be held
- experience tenderness
- know compassion
- make an impact
- mother/father a child
- feel understood
- belong
- give love
- be loved
- experience sexual intimacy
- have security

- be of value
- feel connected

The result of not receiving any one of these longings is loss. What we sometimes forget is that there will be as many losses as there are unmet needs!

Generally these longings, and their consequent losses, can be grouped into three areas:

1. Relationship
2. Family
3. Friendship

Let's take a glimpse at these areas and then go on to look at what is involved in facing longings and handling loss.

Relationship

Perhaps the most obvious and most stated longing for the single person is relationship with the opposite sex – dating, engagement and marriage. The longing for relationship has many facets: to have a partner; to be a pair; to feel valued; to have a role; to be the most important person to someone else; to be what society dictates as the 'norm'. It is easy for onlookers to point out to a struggling single that he/she should be grateful for having *many* friends, but to the single this fails to make up for the fact of not being *the most special person* to any one particular person.

Relationship is to have someone with whom to share the good and the bad times; to know intimacy and closeness; to feel cherished and loved. How the body and mind ache for this state! People say they feel complete, mature, fulfilled when they are 'in love'. Experience tells me that all of these are a reality, and yet another kind of experience tells me that such feelings can be attained in others ways too. At times, though not all the time, I have felt complete, mature and fulfilled through my writing, speaking, helping hurting people, in my friendships and faith. But there is no doubt that courting couples are whisked off into another dimension of living! For the single person who is not dating, observing the starry eyes, cuddles and gracious giving of the courting couple creates an agonising longing and an even more agonising sense of loss.

Within marriage there are the special moments that, as a single person, you dream about; little acts of intimacy and caring which seem so remote. I remember someone talking about how she and her husband would occasionally wake up about four o'clock in the morning and share tea and croissants in bed because neither could sleep. As a single person there is no one to share with at this time and certainly no one to make the tea. Waking at 4.00 a.m. usually means a long and lonely wait until 'morning'!

Relationship can be a wonderful thing, as can marriage I've no doubt, but it is easy for the single person to see it through rose-tinted spectacles, without the rough edges and hard work. Married people all too often remind singles of the fact that marriage is, at times, no bed of roses. But life for the single has its thorny moments too! 'At least the married person, has someone who cares about him/her deeply', the single person thinks, 'and someone to snuggle up to on a cold night'. At times it seems to the single person that all he/she has is an empty bed and the feeling of an empty heart.

Besides loss being experienced through not having a partner, loss is also encountered by the breakdown of relationship – splitting up, ending an engagement, separation and divorce. The pain and loss involved in the break-up of a marriage, engagement or relationship can run deep. Hurtful words and actions may contribute to the disintegration, leaving one or both parties undermined and fearful of trusting again. Whether there has been any unpleasantness in the break-up or not, there is a loss in moving from a partnership to two separate states. Other losses and forms of pain in relationships can include situations such as the single person watching someone he/she has come to love 'go out' with someone else. It is also painful forgoing marriage because you believe that it is wrong to marry a non-Christian (due to the Bible's teaching on not being unequally yoked).

The loss of a partner from death throbs through one's whole being, and in some cases erodes a person's confidence. So often other people rush the process of recovery, try to fill the void, or are embarrassed and don't know what to say. Marcelle lost her husband when she was in her mid-sixties. On a number of occasions she recalls having watched as friends crossed the road so that they did not have to talk to her. Their avoidance through awkwardness only added to her pain.

People rush around and help the widower or widow in the early days and then seem to 'drop' the person. As a result of the loss he/she can feel like a 'half-person' or a 'non-person'. John Bowlby, well known for his research and writing regarding attachment and loss, describes the loss of a loved person as 'one of the most intensely painful experiences any human being can suffer'.[2] 'When the loved figure is believed to be *temporarily* absent the response is one of *anxiety;* when he or she appears to be *permanently* absent it is one of pain and *mourning*.[3]

Whatever the circumstances of losing a partner, there will be a period of adjustment to a new life. Living alone after years of being with someone and a loss of identity in no longer being part of a couple are not easy. So many other issues may need to be faced too, especially where children are involved.

Family

Longings in connection with family involve both the longing to be a part of a family and the longing to have one's own family.

Whilst there can be great pleasure in spending time with families, it can also evoke tremendous pain. Seeing families sharing and caring can remind someone of what was lacking in his/her childhood family, or it can accentuate what is now missing through not being part of a couple and a parent. It can be painful spending time with families when you haven't accepted your current state of singleness. Going back a number of years, I can remember many a night leaving a cosy family home to return alone to my shared accommodation, to find my flat mates out or fast asleep with doors tightly closed. However kind the family I'd visited was, there had to come the time when I would leave whilst they carried on.

I recently talked with a woman in her eighties who lost her husband several years ago. She also finds returning home after being with a family very difficult and puts off going out in order to avoid the dreaded return. What she most needs is someone to go home with her and stay until she has 'settled'. For many singles the leaving creates a sinking feeling which is difficult to define. Only as the person becomes more accepting of him/herself and finds greater satisfaction in life does it become less painful to leave behind the family scene for 'home alone'.

The desire to have children can be overwhelming, especially for women who long to carry and give birth to a baby. The concept of a child growing inside one's body, the feeling of it kicking, and the idea of breastfeeding the baby can leave women feeling extremely broody and bereft. How do you share with someone the flood of grief, the feeling of being robbed, when you long to carry a child but can't because you have no husband? People understand the pain of the childless *married* woman but belittle the pain of the childless *single* woman. 'But you can't feel like that, you're not married.' Her body, whether she is married or not, is still made to carry a child, and at times it feels as if it cries out to be fulfilled. The single woman can long to give birth and she can view giving birth as the ultimate in human fulfilment. Tied in with the desire to have a child is the need to nurture, protect and give.

Although childlessness is painful for women who are still of child-bearing age, there is at least the hope (and even the vague belief) that it may 'still happen'. But for women who start to move beyond their child-bearing years their physical and hormonal state becomes a painful reminder of the ultimate reality. As one woman who had recently undergone a hysterectomy realised, her potential to have children had moved from *probably* no children to *definitely* no children, and it stirred up very strong feelings. We can so easily associate a hysterectomy with the woman who has had her family and has come to the end of that era but not with the woman who has never been in the position to conceive. It can be painful both for women who have had a family and for those who have not.

The loss encountered through not having a family can also be experienced by men. In addition to the desire to parent a child, for some men there is the pressure to carry on the family line. For both sexes there can be longings for a 'complete' experience of oneness with a partner and for nurturing. Perhaps we deny men their feelings of loss by assuming that the childlessness issue belongs only to women.

The single person can gain through giving to other people's children, caring for children who are underprivileged, or sponsoring a child in a Third Word country. I was a nanny for three years and my duties included caring for a newborn baby, which met some of my maternal needs. I have also found it rewarding having my godsons to stay. I have worked with underprivileged children in England, sick children in Africa, and have sponsored various children in Third World countries. But none of the experiences with other people's children or of helping underprivileged children can entirely replace the desire to be a mother.

Harriet, a woman of forty-two, wrote to me about the pain she felt concerning her desire to be a mother. She is the youngest of eight children; her oldest sister had already had a child by the time she was born. She now has twelve nieces and nephews, and fifteen great-nieces and great-nephews! The abundance of children and the special relationship she shares with them allows her to express her maternal feelings and brings much fulfilment. But as Harriet explained:

> There are still some times when I feel so lonely, empty and unfulfilled and would desperately love to have a partner to love and care for, and someone who would care for me too. The longing for children hasn't ceased one bit either. One morning, just before Christmas, I experienced a very real grief reaction when reading about coping with childlessness. I sobbed my heart out and had such a sense of loss it was almost overwhelming. It was also very cathartic, as I haven't felt quite so "broody" since!

Catherine, who is in her seventies, mentioned how not having married and had children has affected her: 'My married friends now have grandchildren, and as we all face old age it seems they have some "investment" in the future; there is the visible evidence of "new life". For me it feels quite different, somewhat desolate; moving towards an ending.'

Friendship

Friendship is different from relationship, because it does not include the romantic or sexual aspects, but the rewards of friendship, the longings and the losses can also run deep for the single person.

There is a longing for connection, to be understood, to feel cared for and to care, to share, and to have meaningful conversation. Life is so much more bearable when one has good friendships; beauty becomes breathtaking and suffering becomes bearable. Some of life's most treasured moments are between friends. True friendships do not collapse with time or distance: years become yesterdays. I waited six years to see some of my friends in South Africa again, and it was as though we had spoken only days ago.

Friendships bring tremendous fulfilment and so when a friendship is broken or is lost it can create a searing pain and emptiness. There can be deep loss when a close friend marries and starts moving in 'couple' circles: the friendship as two single people is now gone. Often even the friendship disintegrates as the single person is 'forgotten'. Sometimes there is guardedness on the part of the newly-married person, in case you 'steal their other half'. Or there may simply be lack of thought because they lose the sense of what it is like to be single. Someone who is married, or even someone who is dating, can easily have little awareness of the longing that a single person has for physical contact, especially to be hugged. Someone once said that we need four hugs a day for survival, eight for maintenance and twelve for growth![4]

For older singles or those faced with tragic circumstances there can be a special sense of loss as they watch their friends and relatives die with the knowledge that they are alone in the world. For some there comes a day when they have no relatives left at all. I was with a woman of seventy one day who said that she was attending her fourth funeral that week. Imagine the feeling of loss she was experiencing; losing one person is painful enough!

Facing longings

Why do we go through life with such intense longings? For the single person the longings mostly tend to become focused on one thing: a marriage partner. Perhaps our longings have a lot to do with how we have been brought up to believe (or have perceived) life would be. Young children start to play 'weddings' and 'mummies' and daddies', as though growing up, getting married and having children is the only path in life. A person can grow up assuming that getting married and having a family will take place without much effort. As the years go by and there seems no evidence, let alone hope, it can leave one feeling disillusioned with life itself. As Jocelyn describes:

> Sometimes I really wonder what this is all about. I grew up expecting to go to university, graduate, work for a couple of years, get married and have children. It hasn't happened.
>
> At university I always seemed to fancy the boys who didn't fancy me, and the ones who fancied me I wasn't interested in! I went out with a couple of guys when I was a student on the occasional date, which I always assumed was platonic. I got a huge shock when, just before my finals, a good friend proposed to me, having broken off with his fiancée. I had never felt attracted to him and had to say 'No'. I lost his friendship.
>
> I went to work abroad for a year after graduating and spent a lot of time wondering if men were worth it. I wondered if I was to be a spinster missionary doomed to return home every few years to give slide shows. That was until the love of my life walked through the door. I felt very attracted to him but he

> wasn't in England very long. We began corresponding. Then one day he just stopped writing. I heard on the grapevine that he had become 'serious' with a girl he had known for years. A year later he got in touch explaining that he had been seeing someone else but it had ended. The relationship seemed to be on and off. One minute he was talking about marriage, the next saying he didn't find me physically attractive (despite having said that I occupied much of his thoughts during his previous relationship).
>
> He was a wonderful guy and in some ways I couldn't believe that someone so special could want to marry me. But another part of me can't believe that I have been let down so badly and that all this went on for so long. I am now left wondering if I have wasted five years of my life and missed my chance of marriage.

The longing for a partner and a family can cause a single person to rush into engagement and marriage, feeling that this might be the only chance. A big fear can be the fear of being 'left on the shelf', and the need to be married may outweigh the 'rightness' of the potential marriage. Some single people feel 'at last here is someone who truly wants me and even if things niggle it *must* be "right".' After all, it is so nice to be wanted, needed and treasured. They say love blinds, that is being 'in love', and so knowing the suitability of a partner for marriage means looking beyond being 'in love'.

The longings and the 'pull' to have a life-partner can be very intense. I know the destructiveness of the 'pull' and how it interferes with one's whole life, where all thinking and most actions seem to revolve around 'finding someone'. I would never belittle how important 'finding someone' is for an individual, but thoughts of tomorrow should not be at the expense of today. Regarding the desire for marriage, I found Anne Atkins' advice, in the book *Split Image*, very helpful:

> ... falling in love is not something you can ever plan. So plan to stay single. Aim to stand firm. One day you may be swept off your feet and your plans will have to change ... you may often feel frustrated or resentful and wish you could be married ... This is natural. In fact it is probably far more common than feeling satisfied and grateful for singleness. We are created to make love, so most single people will feel sexually frustrated. We are created to have children, so many single (and some married) people will feel their parental instincts are being frustrated. And we are created to be in partnership with the opposite sex, so single people – particularly in our 'nuclear family' society – may often feel unsettled or lonely without the lifelong commitment of marriage. What we often tend to forget is that everyone is frustrated. We are also made to work, so the unemployed are frustrated. We are made to subdue the earth, so the powerless are frustrated ... It is foolish to pretend we are not frustrated, but it is equally foolish to forget that everyone else is frustrated too.[5]

We all have longings but one of the hardest things of allowing our longings to dictate to us is that unpredictability in our lives seems to lead to insecurity. Allowing our longings to haunt and dictate does nothing for us. We need to accept longings for what they are – unfulfilled desires which may, or may not, one day be fulfilled. We then need to get in touch with the loss which is attached and allow it to be a part of our personal growth. It sounds easy, but from first-hand experience I know it isn't!

Handling loss

Some people don't really think of their experiences as encompassing loss. Barbara Ward, who has worked for many years in bereavement counselling, and who lost her husband in an accident just nine months after they were married, said:

> Each time we make a change in our lives, take on a new role or let go of an old one, we experience loss. You have to lose the old in order to make room for the new. Our culture is so focused on the gains we can make in life – a new relationship, a new job, a new home, a new family – that the inevitable accompanying loss is rarely considered. We expect ourselves to adapt to any change swiftly; to 'carry on as usual'.[6]

Does grieving over not marrying seem strange? I know for myself there have been moments when I have grieved very deeply. We even find an account of such grieving in the Bible – Jephthah's daughter. She said to her father: '*... let me go up into the hills and roam with my girlfriends for two months, weeping because I'll never marry*' (Judges 11:37 TLB). *Her father turned to her: '"Yes", he said. "Go". And so she did, bewailing her fate with her friends for two months*' (11:38 TLB).

Some losses will be obvious, such as when a partner dies; a relationship, engagement or marriage breaks up; a child leaves home, etc. Others will be less obvious, such as the grief which arises out of not having had children, and will need to be given thought. When we encounter loss and grief it is helpful to know that a grief process takes time and requires support. Unacknowledged or untackled past loss makes present loss more difficult to handle. Many people have never dealt with childhood losses because these losses have been 'forgotten', or they are so painful that the person fears losing control and not being able to cope in everyday life. One loss becomes added to the previous loss and as soon as you allow yourself to grieve, it is like a flood which gushes forth. We may be afraid of our grief because it seems that once we get in touch with it and begin to allow it out, it will just keep on coming and literally drown us.

When a person fails to get in touch with his/her loss and does not talk about it openly and honestly it can result in unhelpful behaviour patterns. When Heidi was in her mid-twenties she had a compulsive longing to be hugged. She always wanted hugs to be given by a middle-aged woman. The need became so great that Heidi would take herself to the Samaritans and, once there, she would ask to see a woman. She would hide her face and act helpless, hurting and much younger than she really was. The child in her, who had not bonded with her mother, was crying out for a 'mother figure' or what John Bowlby calls an 'attachment figure'. Because there was a disturbance in the development of attachment, when she reached adulthood she was, without realising, trying to fulfil something which actually was lacking in childhood. In order to break free from the pattern of constantly wanting affirmation from an older woman she had to face her loss in childhood, grieve for what had been missing, and then let go.

Another consequence of the failure to get in touch with loss and to work through it is depression. In Chapter 1, I mentioned how unexpressed anger can lead to depression. This anger may often come as a result of loss in childhood. Loss in childhood can include the physical or emotional absence of a parent, or any trauma. From my observations and interpretation of my own experience, it seems that there is a process which takes place: loss in childhood which has not been worked through, longing for closeness which goes unfulfilled, internalised anger, defensive reactions which go unrecognised, difficulty in maintaining or feeling close in relationships.

John Bowlby explains the connection between loss in childhood, difficulty in maintaining relationships, and depression:

In most forms of depressive disorder, including that of chronic mourning, the principal issue about which a person feels helpless is his ability to make and to maintain affectional relationships. The feeling of being helpless in these particular regards can be attributed, I believe, to the experiences he has had in his family of origin. These experiences, which are likely to have continued well into adolescence, are postulated to have been of one, or some combination of three interrelated kinds:

a. He is likely to have had the bitter experience of never having attained a stable and secure relationship with his parents despite having made repeated efforts to do so, including having done his utmost to fulfil their demands and perhaps also the unrealistic expectations they may have had of him. These childhood experiences result in his developing a strong bias to interpret any loss he may later suffer as yet another of his failures to make or maintain a stable affectional relationship.
b. He may have been told repeatedly how unlovable, and/or how inadequate, and/or how incompetent he is. (A common motive for a parent, usually a mother, to speak to a child or adolescent in this kind of way is to ensure that he remains at home to care for her ... Most misleadingly, pressure of this kind is often mistaken for 'overprotection'). Were he to have had these experiences they would result in his developing a model of himself as unlovable and unwanted, and a model of attachment figures as likely to be unavailable, or rejecting, or punitive. Whenever such a person suffers adversity, therefore, so far from expecting others to be helpful he expects them to be hostile and rejecting.
c. He is more likely than others to have experienced actual loss of a parent during childhood with conse-

> quences to himself that, however disagreeable they might have been, he was impotent to change. Such experiences would confirm him in the belief that any effort he might make to remedy his situation would be doomed to failure.[7]

The single person who can identify with this process so often looks to the desire for marriage, or relationship, as the reliever of the 'pain' rather than understanding and sorting out the roots of the hurt.

Betrayal

Along with loss there can be a feeling of betrayal, especially for the person who did not initiate a relationship's break-up, or for the one left behind following the death of a partner. There may also be a feeling of not being complete. This is especially true for those who are going through, or have gone through, separation or divorce.

> Many people who go through a divorce do not give themselves the emotional space to grieve fully. It is common to deny the full reality of such a loss by refusing to see the positive aspects of the relationship you have lost; or to stay stuck in anger or guilt. If you suppress your sadness to stay in control, you add to your stress. If you don't keep moving through the stages of grief, you won't ever leave your old relationship emotionally, and are likely to sabotage future relationships by unconsciously bringing all your old emotional baggage into them.[8]

Feelings come in a mixed bunch when you lose someone through the break-up of a relationship: shock, relief, failure, anger, guilt and sadness can all pour over the person, leaving him/her wondering what on earth is going on and how he/she will ever cope again.

What takes place in the loss/grief process?

> The first three stages of the transition curve relate to various stages of grief, beginning with *immobilisation* ('shock and disbelief'), then *minimisation* ('denial'), and *self-doubt/depression* ('depression'). The low-point of the self-esteem curve is *acceptance/letting* go. This is not the peaceful acceptance that completes the stages of grief, but rather the step out of denial. Once the reality of the loss is accepted, the curve of self-esteem rises through *testing* (trying out new ways of being), and *search for meaning,* until at *internalisation,* self-esteem has returned to the level it was at before the loss.[9]

When we work through loss and move on, it is important to *talk* and to *cry*. 'Emotional tears play a precise and central role in helping to restore the chemical balance of the body by excreting substances produced by the body in response to stress.'[10] Dr William Frey discovered that 'the lacrimal gland, which regulates tear secretion, concentrates and removes manganese from the body. The concentration of manganese, a mineral affecting mood alteration, is thirty times greater in tears than in blood serum. He also found that emotional tears have a different chemical makeup from irritant tears.[11]

We have to give ourselves permission to grieve. We need to know that it's OK to feel that way and to express it. In order to heal well we also need to be kind to ourselves; to recognise that we may have to take things easy. Loss often knocks a person's self-esteem and erodes their ability to handle life. At a time of loss it is also not unusual to feel unloved.

As well as giving ourselves permission to grieve following the ending of a relationship we have to create a 'closure'. It has been pointed out that:

> If you are divorced, you may intellectually realise that the marriage is over while not at all letting go of it

> emotionally. Since there is no funeral or closure-oriented decision such as burying a loved one, you may find it difficult to bury the marriage ... We need closure if we want to get well, and closing an expectation is even more difficult when the person associated with that loss expectation still walks the earth ... One goal in Grief Release is to withdraw the emotional energy we had invested in the relationship we lost by learning how to say goodbye to the relationship as it existed and can never exist again.[12]

Whether the closure is due to an end in marriage, engagement or relationship makes no difference. When my engagement ended several months ago I went to see a counsellor who helped me to create an ending by suggesting I carry out a ritual. I wrote down my deepest thoughts and feelings and found a beautifully tranquil spot where a friend and I sat and prayed. I then read the writings for the final time and burnt them. It brought about a release in me which was symbolic of 'letting go'; this was followed by enjoyment in going out for a nice meal. I experienced the importance of creating an ending, which was observed by another person and included receiving affirmation from that person. Just like in a burial, where there are people gathered and there is a point in ending, such a transition has to take place to move on to the next phase.

I have experienced loss in many forms and circumstances including pets, my own home, my job, relationships, two engagements, and the loss of friends and relations through natural death, suicide and murder. Not long ago I had three major losses all in the space of a couple of months: job, home (and cat), and engagement. I had many of the marriage plans in process and had already bought the dress, bridesmaid's and pageboy's material. I found myself thrown into a strange and acutely painful world. Lack of confidence, pain, sorrow and anxiety crashed over me in waves. Battered and breathless I emerged for air before being swept away again and finding myself beaten on the rocks. And yet I questioned why I felt so bad. My GP at the time commented that one bereavement was enough for anyone: 'You have suffered three in close succession which is more than the human psyche can take'. He said that what I most needed was a support system: close friends around, with whom I could cry.

It made me think about the whole concept of support and how, sadly, a system is often lacking. *Support* means to 'carry all or part of the weight of; keep from falling or sinking or failing'. Also 'enable to last out; give strength to; encourage', and 'give help or countenance to, backup'. *System* means 'an organised body of material or immaterial things'. Other words used to describe it include group, network, and structure.[13]

Support system

A support system is a group of somebodies who love us and will come alongside us to help sustain the stressful load caused by grief. A support system consists of a network of people, usually two to ten, who have committed themselves to lend a hand in practical ways … A support system will help stabilise you by functioning as a sounding board.[14]

If we all had a good support system we would be better able to cope with the losses and struggles in life. But we need to remember that it is not only a question of needing a support system, but finding one. A large part of the finding is *our* responsibility. My experience is that if you are willing to support others and people see this level of care as an example, and you are willing to show your vulnerability, support will follow. If it doesn't, we need to learn to ask!

I have had periods in my life where I have not had a good support system in the vicinity, but more recently I have had an excellent support system. I have also been a support to a number of people – gone out to friends who are hurting in the middle of the night and sat with them and listened. When we have a support system it is necessary to know what our needs are, so that we can ascertain the kind of support we require: sometimes it is company, at other times a hug, at other times the chance to talk about how we feel. Sometimes we need professional support.

In our quest for support we must also recognise that there are moments when there is no support and the lack of it will either drive us towards self-destruction or drive us closer to God. Larry Crabb, founder of the Institute of Biblical Counselling in Colorado, asked at a recent seminar: 'Are we using God to solve our problems or are we using our problems to find God?' He's got a point!

Positives of loss

Loss and the consequent grieving process are regarded by some as purely negative – experiences they wish to be over as soon as possible. In fact loss can be one of the most changing and, in the end, most positive encounters. It is often during a time of loss that we have the opportunity to examine our lives, our priorities, our friendships and our direction. Loss occurs in the context of crisis. The Chinese character (word) for crisis has two parts, meaning 'danger' and 'opportunity'. Grief is about putting together the broken pieces to create something new.

The counsellor I have been consulting since my overload of loss spoke of how I had to grieve and then see the different life which is emerging. The grief involves getting in touch with everything that could have been and how my life might now be if I had married and still been in my job. The new life emerging, because of the crisis, includes a change in direction and something positive being born. I am moving towards contemplating paths which would possibly have remained untrodden had I now been married.

More important, perhaps, is the fact that I have changed. Crisis can transform us. Out of my time of crisis, when I felt that I wanted to shut down completely and had lost hope, has grown something more precious than I ever had before. The horror of the pain, and the care from other people through the pain, is building in me a character change. I feel a more gentle, caring, peaceful person who is able to give and receive love in a different way. The loss of confidence I experienced, and the pulling down of me as a person, initially created times when I felt very negative and self-destructive. Both of these demanded energy and took a great deal out of me. Slowly I have learned to channel that energy in a more constructive way.

The answer is different for each individual but, being creative, I have found that at the times when I feel most down and destructive doing craft or painting pictures of animals helps. Through creative activity I get in touch with my senses and God's creativity, and I bring something to life.

Not having what we long for, and not relinquishing the longings, can set us up for agonising loneliness and inner pain. We have to reach a place of 'letting go'. As I look at my own experience of loss, whether this was the loss of a relationship or the loss encountered through a change in my life, I see endings and beginnings. As one stage ends and another begins, it is only after the latter has begun to develop that I can see the significance of the death of the one for the birth and growth of the other.

4 | *Problems and Practicalities*

Being on your own often means handling the problems and practicalities of life alone. Having someone around, quite apart from what they can do practically, eases the mountain of pain and frustration which can become out of proportion.

Under pressure

Being single does bring pressures – maybe different pressures from those of married people but nevertheless pressure. Those who are in a leadership position, or who are in a position of great responsibility, and have little or no support system, can feel that they have a heavy load to carry on their own. Single people training for the ministry have expressed being fearful of having to handle situations and people without the backup of the love and care of a partner – not that there are any guarantees that a partner will provide the love and care they want! There's no doubting, however, the real support a partner can provide when shouldering a heavy burden: in practical ways, advice or just listening.

Finance can also be a stress for some single people. One woman who has been on 'benefit' for a long time said that she finds it hard to socialise with Christians who have few money worries, and who invite her out for a meal! She has to debate whether to go and spend what would otherwise keep her in food for a week. That hurts! Singles, when setting up home, do not receive wedding presents (which include many household items) as most couples do. Setting up home means finding the money for all those items and that can be financially draining.

For some divorced or separated people financial security goes when their partner goes. Managing the finances becomes like a chain around the neck. Some people, suddenly having to handle the financial side of running a home, find themselves taking on a role they have not had to consider before. My own dislike is the dreaded tax form. The responsibility of filling it in correctly and having to do my sums properly (not my strong point) fills me with gloom. Even worse is the panic-stricken feeling when the request for money arrives and I am not sure if the tax office has assessed me correctly. It is then that I long for someone else to take the responsibility.

What many single people struggle with, when not in a relationship, is lack of moral support. We all need the knowledge that someone is 'rooting' for us. Moral support can be found in friends, not just partners, but the single person so often perceives such things as only being available through a partner. Besides, he/she is always stumbling over couples who have what is longed for, which highlights what is missing.

Mixing and meeting

If you live alone and are shy it can be a real effort to meet others. One can go for days without socialising, maybe weeks without touch. Singles frequently find themselves having to initiate any discussion about their situation. What if one finds it difficult to initiate? Going to places alone where you are expected to mix with others, especially for the more reserved person, can be painful and requires courage. One widow I spoke to said that she found it particularly hard going to functions alone. 'If people would only go with me instead of saying "I'll see you there", it would really help.' Invitations to functions are often addressed to you plus 'one other' which usually means a husband/wife or partner. What if the person has no 'other'? Instead there is an increased sense of aloneness. Some singles feel that they are invited merely to 'make up the numbers'. Even walking into a church alone and trying to find someone to sit with can fill some people with dread. And sitting with another person doesn't alter the fact that you are single!

We have to make time for relating if we are going to meet a variety of people and increase the chances of meeting that special someone we may feel comfortable with in a long-term relationship or marriage. I used to moan about not having met the right person, but at the same time most days I was nose to the grindstone morning to night. Did I suddenly expect someone to input 'Mr Right' on the computer system and see if I could squeeze him into my diary?

Where a single person's life is centred around a particular club, activity or the church, a feeling of 'limited opportunities' and a fear that they will never meet anyone can arise. As one young man stated somewhat bluntly: 'There are only a limited number of people of the opposite sex; and more than one guy might have their eye on the same girl!' For a good social life and the chance to meet people it is necessary to pursue getting to know people in a variety of contexts and to be prepared to mix with people who may be different from you – different cultures, different social classes, different interests, different races, different ages, professionals and non-professionals.

Some singles devote their time and energy into looking after elderly parents and suddenly in mid-life, following the death of their parents, find themselves thrust into an empty world. For years they had a purpose and their life consisted of a routine. They had no need, time or perhaps chance to socialise. Equally, some widows have talked of how, having been married for years and with their life having revolved around couples, when their partner died they were the odd one out. Death itself brought emptiness and an intensity of feelings, and now there are added difficulties in relating. Within marriage they may have formed their identity around their partner rather than individually, and suddenly they must re-create. The thought of going out or making new friends can be daunting.

Another problem for those who have lost a partner (due to death, divorce or separation) is the sudden change of not having someone with whom to share responsibility, someone off whom to bounce ideas. This can be felt especially acutely when there are children to raise. The person can be left asking: 'Am I making the right decision?' Claudia, whose husband died when she was thirty-two, talked of having the 'I-Don't-Know' Syndrome. Throughout her married life of twelve years she had been used to asking her husband how she looked and what she should wear when going out. Suddenly she found herself changing two or three times before leaving the house, completely unsure of herself.

When a partnership ends and a person is left on his/her own there is a great deal to cope with: feelings and hurts, everyday household work, earning an income, practical issues and, for some people, raising a family. It is a time when sensitivity and support are needed. But as Jan, who was left on her own to raise four children and support herself, said:

> When I most needed practical help and support, having been used to two of us doing the work, one of the church leaders was critical because I didn't turn up for a meeting. How could I go with piles of ironing, four children to sort out for school, to say nothing of how I was feeling emotionally following a traumatic break-up with my husband?

Assumptions

For the person who has been married and for the person who has never been married, there can be the desire to mix with married people, and yet they can feel a disturbing niggling doubt as to whether they are really wanted. Singles can easily make assumptions about marrieds: that they are too busy, can't be bothered or are only interested in socialising with other marrieds and their children. When I talked to some married friends about this they said they welcomed singles coming round so long as they could take the family as they found them and didn't expect them to drop everything. One interesting comment from a married woman was that her children become difficult when she engages in conversation with another person for long periods. The children compete for attention and it is important that, at times, they are included. This means that the single person must be sensitive to the needs of the children as well.

Marrieds also make assumptions about singles. 'They won't want to visit with my kids around; it might be too noisy or demanding!' 'We can't drop in on our single friends because something's bound to get broken'. Yet many singles wish that marrieds would drop in occasionally – children and all. But dropping in can be stressful for the married with young children who, upon entering a non-childproof home, demolish everything destructible in seconds. I have learned that if I want marrieds with children to visit me, I must be prepared to lift breakables above toddler height and keep a few toys in store. It just goes to show that what is most needed between marrieds and singles is *communication*.

The feeling that married people are too busy to bother can cause much grief for single people. Georgina, who is in her twenties, has often talked to me about a painful encounter which has repeated itself many times. A married woman befriended her in her time of need and she was encouraged to come to the house at any time. However, the husband was always dropping hints that the wife had spent enough time already. When Georgina phoned, the husband gave the impression that the wife was too busy. In the end, because she tried to help too many people, the wife *was* too busy, and in a time of great need Georgina was left alone. Now she feels too scared to make contact.

Problems can also sometimes occur when a single person is friendly with a married couple and one of the partners feels threatened by the single person. It can hurt when these feelings are not talked about in a mature way and the single person is left 'feeling the vibes'. There is responsibility on both sides: the married person has a responsibility to be in a secure marriage and to air any concerns; and the single person has the responsibility to ensure that he/she does not cause disruption to a marriage, or dominate the time of one partner.

Parenting alone

There are added problems for single parents. There may be a lack of practical and financial support in bringing up a child; lack of input from the other parent (which is needed for a child's emotional health); lack of ability to work as a team; lack of anyone to talk to about the needs of the children. Thoughts, such as, 'What would happen to the children if I ceased coping?' crop up. Then there can be the feeling of uselessness which may arise when the children leave home. The children have been companions, the reason for structure and, for some single parents, even the reason for living. Suddenly the way ahead seems very bleak.

It can be difficult to bear the weight of raising children single-handed. A parent who is at home with pre-school children and unable to go out much in the evening can crave talking to another adult. One can feel frustrated relating to children all the time. Finding or affording babysitters can be difficult, leaving the parent having to turn down opportunities to socialise. Rhiannon's daughter was five when her father left them. She explains how her social life was affected: 'For at least eighteen months I didn't go far from home. I was so aware of families who were complete with two parents. Many times I would go out and come home very upset. It took me seven years to pluck up the courage to go abroad on holiday.'

Maria, another single mother, overcame the difficulty by forming a group for single, separated and divorced people: 'It was interesting to note that it only attracted women though! I was also supported by the local Relate branch and had babysitters from my Bible study group.'

Though socialising may have its harder moments, dating is generally more difficult. It may not be easy for a single parent to get out to meet people, and when he/she does meet someone they need to be accepting of the fact that children are part of the picture. The children sometimes find dating threatening, especially as some children have a fantasy about their parents getting back together. Children also still need attention and could be jealous or hurt when that attention is divided. Even for the non-custodial parent there can be pressures. Some prospective partners are put off by the fact that the person has been previously married, and even more so by the fact that there are children.

Although we tend to speak about single mothers, we need to remember that the parent given custody of the children is sometimes the father. That said, most often it is the father who is left on his own with limited visiting time with his children. The partner who is separated from his/her children has the practical problems of the non-custodial parent. Maybe a visit to the children involves a long journey in a busy life. Do we ever consider their pain and frustration? In what way can we help? It is too easy to think of the single parent with the children and ignore the single parent without the children.

Heights of joy to depths of despair

Relationships, dating, breaking up, falling for someone who hasn't fallen for you, are also pressure points for the single person. The single person so often finds him/herself thrown from the heights of joy to the depths of despair in a split second. People underestimate the pain caused in a relationship which ends or doesn't go smoothly. It is difficult to cut off from the pain in everyday life, and yet the single person must often work to earn a living. It is easy to feel disillusioned, especially since the movies portray 'falling in love' so differently from the way it usually works out in practice!

For many single people the end of a relationship is yet another rejection. Others are able to see it in a different light: broken relationships, struggles and hurts are not failures *in* life but teach us *about* life. We do well to learn from falling into a pattern of choosing relationships which are not productive for us. When a relationship breaks down, perhaps we should ask ourselves two questions:

- What have I learned about myself?
- What have I learned about the kind of person who is suitable for me?

We need to look at, and possibly change, our beliefs about relationships and marriage expectations. There are several fairytales which as children we believe in, and as adults we hold on to. Girl meets prince and they live happily ever after. For many adults the fairytale becomes an illusion which we place onto a relationship. The illusion is like a bubble. When we pass the 'love blinds' phase of the relationship the bubble bursts and we come face to face with the person we are dating: the dark and the light. To know whether this is the 'right' person is to know that we can live with what we find.

When a relationship, especially one which was on the

path to marriage, breaks up, saying goodbye to the prince (the person we have been dating or have been engaged to) means saying goodbye to the principality (the chance for children, a home, a married life). That is partly why a broken engagement is so acutely painful: the experience feels more painful due to the need to say goodbye to all the hopes attached to the person.

Following a break-up people need time to re-adjust to life and to rebuild confidence. A person who has been in a dating relationship needs to slot back into the life of not having anyone special. A divorced or separated person can be in conflict, not just with his/her ex-partner but morally and spiritually. The children of the divorced or separated person require stability and love. Now is the time when all these people need understanding and care.

Whilst some singles have reached an end in relationship, and need care, others may be at the point of starting a relationship, or are confused over where things are going, and need a sounding board. When you are single and start talking to a single person of the opposite sex that person could assume you fancy them, or all the interested onlookers do!

What do you do if you genuinely want to be friends with someone but do not want to date them? Or, they just want to be friends with you but you are desperately hoping there will be more to it? Things can so easily become entangled and result in one or both parties being hurt. Both people, from the beginning, would be wise to express honestly any needs, thoughts and feelings regarding the friendship. As people talk about how they feel there is less likelihood of misunderstanding. Men and women often interpret things somewhat differently and so it is necessary to know each other's expectations and boundaries. It is so easy to hear what you *want* to hear rather than what is *actually* being said, and to confuse the rejection of a relationship with the rejection of the person.

Who's right?

Not knowing when and how to say 'no' to relationships can be difficult. We don't always know what type of person is suitable for us and can enter into relationship after relationship with the wrong type of person. Many of us say that we want marriage and yet, have we ever really thought about what kind of person is best suited to us? What do we need in that person – intellectually, spiritually, emotionally and socially? Knowing what we need can help to prevent entering dead-end relationships. Susan Page, author of *If I'm so Wonderful Why Am I Still Single*? suggests a strategy to discover the kind of person we are looking for:

a. On paper, describe your ideal mate. List all the qualities, talents, propensities you'd like him/her to have. 'Brainstorm' with yourself. Take your time and include everything. There is no need to be 'realistic'. Don't censor.
b. Now go back over your list and place either an 'E' for essential or a 'D' for desirable next to each item.
c. List all the 'E' qualities on a separate page in the order of their importance to you.
d. Draw a line under the top five items on the 'E' list.[1]

It wouldn't be appropriate in this book to talk about how to develop a relationship and why a relationship goes wrong (it would take a book in itself and I am still learning!). But if a person finds him/herself entering one relationship after another – which appears to follow a similar pattern – and not getting any nearer marriage, it can be helpful to consider:

- Am I choosing the wrong type of person? If so, why?
- Has my childhood influenced my choice? If so, in what way?
- Are there things in me I need to change?

- Am I prepared to change?
- If I am prepared to change, am I also prepared to realise that what I am looking for in a relationship might be quite different?

How can we begin to overcome the fear of being hurt again, and consider getting close? Harold Ivan Smith, who has led many seminars in the USA for single adults, explains:

1. ***Consider your best interests***. If you live your life based on fear, you may live the rest of your life alone. Do you really want to do that? It is always in your best interest to grow.
2. ***Examine your choices***. If you stop dating; if you become a workaholic; if you pour yourself into hobbies, your children or civic programmes, then you may be running away from your problems and not working on resolving them. Flight tends to stimulate fear and fright.
3. ***Anticipate your future***. God wants you to have a great future. But look ahead five or ten years. If you embrace your fear by continuing to nourish it, you will lose many opportunities to experience love. Taking risks is a basic part of life. Honestly admit your fears. Then take steps to move on with your life in spite of them.
4. ***Appraise your needs and expectations***. Exaggerating your needs or trying to 'make up for lost time' is another way of avoiding being hurt. You have a right to have expectations of a relationship. But be careful about unrealistic needs that will cause you to idealise some relationships and avoid others.
5. ***Give yourself time***. You have plenty of time to rebuild and to heal. You are not ready for the future until you have finished the business of the past. Time is one luxury that you can afford during this period.

6. ***Recognise that if you want satisfying relationships you will have to work at them.*** Are you making choices that result in repeated hurt and rejection? Do you always blame the other person? What changes can you make in your own behaviour that could make a difference?
7. ***Admit your fears verbally.*** That way the person you are dating has at least been put on notice and may be more appreciative of your fears.[2]

Overcoming the fear of being hurt again relieves a certain amount of pressure and this is easily understood by others, whatever their marital status. Perhaps less understood by people who have chosen to spend the rest of their lives together are the frustrations which can be associated with living arrangements.

Living arrangements

Living arrangements can be a challenge for the single person. Do you live alone and risk loneliness, or share a house and risk not getting on with the people? If you live alone you may be the one always having to go out to see people. What if no one comes and visits you and the home becomes a little prison? If you share a house, how do the bills work out? You might be someone who doesn't like to waste electricity whilst your flat-mates think nothing of it. There might be constant noise and clutter or invasion of privacy.

Kathy Keay's experience of shared accommodation says it all: 'People say you get all the rough corners knocked off you which would otherwise be knocked off in marriage, but in my experience it's the mugs and plates which get chipped first, and there's usually one person with Natural Charisma or Delegated Authority who keeps an eye on things and makes sure you take your turn on the washing-up rota.'[3]

Personally, I have tried several varieties of accommodation and have come to the conclusion that each has its pros and cons and none seems ideal! I started off in a bed-sit in a seedy part of town. It was 'home' because I made it such, but one could hardly entertain in the room which was bedroom, sitting room, dining room and kitchen. My neighbours, who were drunk most of the time, taught me little other than how to fiddle electricity meters, and most of my friends seemed more frightened to enter the place than free to pop in. In many respects it was lonely. I had no TV or telephone. The bathroom was shared, and I stumbled over semi-conscious bodies in the night, but I loved painting the walls and it was my bid at independence whilst still a teenager.

After picking myself up out of a hole and a spell back at home (never easy when you've already left), I graduated to house-sharing. You'd think you wouldn't be lonely with others around, but at times we would be like ships passing in the night and did not see each other for days. Scraps of paper with scribbled notes became the new form of communication. When we did see each other at least there was company, and there was a TV! But I couldn't easily entertain because it wasn't mine; I certainly couldn't paint the walls; and cleaning rotas drove me mad.

Then came living with families. Usually there was a TV *and* a video *and* a dishwasher (or, in my South African days, a maid) *and* often meals provided. In many ways it was luxury with my own shower-room. It was a home, but not mine, and I was conscious of my every move. I still couldn't entertain and, in one place, crying babies kept me awake!

At last came the much-longed-for solution – a house of my own. I spent hours wallpapering, painting, putting up shelves and creating a pine haven. I even had a little garden which I landscaped and in which I grew my own strawberries, lettuces and tomatoes amongst the flowers. It was a real home, not just for me but for two cats. My cats added entertainment with their manic behaviour and company with their cuddles. Having my own home brought satisfaction and an outlet for my nesting and creative instincts. Bliss! It had a TV and eventually a video, and I could watch what I wanted when I wanted. I could soak in the bath for hours and leave my paper-work spread on the floor. But being on my own did mean that I paid the price of loneliness at times; and owning my own property meant that I was financially crippled! Financially crippled or not, owning one's own home does give a sense of dignity.

After four years the house went on the market because I was getting married. It was sold and I felt bereft. Then my engagement ended and I found myself renting a room in a new town with new people. My heart ached for my former home and the cats I had left behind. But soon my new room became my home, with as much of my furniture crammed in as would fit. It was a sitting-room and office by day and bedroom by night. I became a part of a family, who had knocked two houses into one and juggled an assortment of lodgers which became busier than Victoria station. (Since writing this book I have mostly lived on the job – communal living as part of a charity. This has its ups and downs! I am discovering the importance of having one's own space wherever one lives and establishing a sense of identity in the living accommodation even if only one room!).

If fortunate enough to have a place of one's own, it is important to use home-making instincts and create a place which reflects one's personality and is open to visitors – warm and welcoming. Our homes should be an extension of ourselves, not just a house or flat; somewhere where we open the door to ourselves and allow other people to get to know us. As a single person living alone, or in a room in rented accommodation, it is easy to walk into a family home and immediately feel the beauty and warmth, the busyness and interaction of relationships. Going back into one's own accommodation the single person can feel a comparative coldness and emptiness. But even the most basic accommodation can be made into a home with a little effort and imagination, as David Mansell describes:

> The very word "bedsitter" seems to have an in-built feeling of loneliness – spending the evening alone staring at four blank walls. We must rid ourselves of the idea that the place where we eat and sleep is simply where we end up by force of circumstances when we having nothing to do, nowhere to go and no one to see.
>
> Your home must not be viewed as merely temporary:
>
> - a pause between activities
> - a waiting-room for marriage
> - a stop-gap until you get a 'real home'
> - a place to camp for the night
>
> The attitude that a person's home doesn't have real and permanent value today will quickly turn it into a prison of introspection where unhappy memories, regrets and unrealised hopes flood the mind.
>
> No, it isn't your marital status but the kind of person you are that determines the kind of home you can build. *A happy home is the extension of a happy person.*[4]

When it comes to accommodation choice, perhaps our personality comes into the decision. I like to think I coped well on my own, and in many respects I did, but being someone who loves people and is energised and stimulated by their company I now realise that I need to have folk around whom I can pop in on or who will visit me.

Some people can't cope with being alone, and this is no failure but needs to be recognised. For many people, being on their own (whether it is actually living alone or feeling alone because flat mates are not close friends) can create problems. Being alone may mean opening birthday cards alone, handling responsibility alone, buying food alone, being ill alone, coping with a crisis alone, dark evenings alone, and even scary movies alone!

One thing I used to hate was shopping alone, especially as I did not have a car. I worked long hours and would often wait until the cupboards were almost bare before venturing forth. I would set off for the supermarket, the butcher's and the fruit stall with my Mexican bag. Why, when I knew I had to walk back, I would fill the bag so full I'll never know. My arms would stretch; my shoulders ache and my eyes moisten as I made the trek back up the hill. It seemed that every car which zoomed by had a happy hubby, a wonderful wife and 2.4 smiling children.

Many single people say that one of the lowest moments is returning home alone after church on Sunday, knowing that families are eating their roast gathered around a table together. Christmas presents a dilemma – do you return 'home' to Mum and Dad and feel like a child? Pull crackers alone? Hope to be invited by a family (and risk feeling *very single* in their midst)? The end of the working day and the weekend can also fill people with heaviness, or tear them in two directions: looking forward to the free time and fearing the emptiness. Bank Holidays are often the most depressing days for the single person, when he/she waits to see what others are doing and fears being left out.

The dreaded Valentine's Day!

Holidays or other 'special' days can be difficult, as one hopes to be invited or does the inviting but finds that someone else has already asked that particular friend. Mothering Sunday is a traumatic day for many single people who long for children. Some churches have got round this problem by the children presenting *all* the women with flowers or cards. Then there is the ultimate dreaded day: St Valentine's, when there are constant reminders of the fact that the whole world, apart from you, has someone special. The postman arrives and you hope and wonder what the thud on the door mat could mean. It's not so much the fact that you 'haven't got', but rather answering the inevitable question: 'Did you get?'

Last year Valentine's Day brought a huge bouquet of flowers and the beginning of a romance. This year it brought nothing but, for the first time, somehow it didn't matter. I felt loved and cared for by people, and a friend who had received a dozen red roses from her fiancé gave me one. I was very touched that she had thought of me and taken the trouble to share her gift. It was a sign of how cherished good friendships are, even if the longed-for romance doesn't exist.

Doing the DIY

'One of the hardest things about being single is doing jobs alone,' one woman told me. 'It really pulls me down.' When you are in the middle of trying to cope alone with DIY jobs which defeat you, life can suddenly feel like extremely hard work. I remember the day I had twelve foreign students coming to tea at my little house, only really large enough to house myself, two cats and a couple of visitors. The kettle was boiling, I had every mug I owned out, and for some reason I was fiddling with the shower curtain. A huge crash told me that the rail and probably half the plaster had fallen down and at that moment the van drew up outside. As the doorbell rang I was balancing on the bath endeavouring to restore the damage. How I longed for a loving husband to run to my aid as I greeted my guests, poured out the tea and struggled to look in control. Instead of which I stumbled down the stairs looking hot and flustered and covered in debris!

DIY and decorating for some people can be very stressful. Never having learned these arts, having a physical problem which makes certain actions difficult, or being elderly and frail can leave a person feeling a failure or angry and helpless. If you ask the partner of a friend for help you may be viewed with suspicion by some people. Then again, what if you find asking for help difficult? I am pretty resourceful and will try my hand at most things; I am also stubborn and don't like to be defeated so usually get the jobs done!

In the past I would have found it difficult to ask for help if unable to do a certain job, but now I know my limits and who to ask. It can even be fun involving other people. Shortly after I moved to my own home I bought a Welsh dresser. The only problem was that it arrived flat-packed with instructions. Fortunately, the day after it arrived I had invited a family over for a meal. I cooked the meal and afterwards the husband and two young boys volunteered to erect the dresser whilst the wife, young girl and I sat and talked. That's life! It sounds a bit sexist but we all had fun and I had a Welsh dresser!

DIY at my current home creates some of the most entertaining and adrenalin-pumping times. Whether single or married, you don't feel alone in doing the jobs. Recently it was discovered that the two large sofas which had been bought for the first-floor flat wouldn't go up the stairs. Several members of the house helped to remove the entire window of one of the bedrooms, and using a car tow-rope, hauled each sofa up a ladder outside my room. Half way up one of the sofas got stuck on the join in the ladder. One person was left up the ladder with the sofa on his shoulder whilst someone ran to the attic to get another ladder and a piece of wood to create a smooth slide. 'Go carefully' one of the men shouted as more members of the road came out to observe what seemed to be unbelievable. Fortunately, they made it!

In moments of DIY difficulty the cry of the single woman is so often: 'I wish I had a man'. I've screamed it myself when I've pressed a wrong key on the computer and got myself jammed. But even if I had a man he might not know anything about computers! Single, or otherwise, we need to learn to use all the resources available and not live in the fantasy that a partner can rescue us from our plight. And sometimes we have to accept that we don't have the resources within ourselves and that there isn't anyone available to assist. It is then that we must be prepared to pay the price of professional help.

Travel

Another problem of the single life is travel. Travelling alone can be dangerous and can be expensive (the usual single person 'supplements'). One author, writing about living alone as a woman, has called the single person supplement the Noah's Ark Syndrome, 'Because it implies that holidaymakers, like animals in the ark, go two by two.'[5]

Quite apart from safety and expense, travelling is generally more enjoyable with someone else. For many people there exists the need to share and express delight or difficulty with someone they know. I have travelled both alone and with others for holidays. Whilst each has its reward, travelling with someone else generally has been less stressful, and there is the joy of recapturing the special moments in conversation. Some single people may find themselves reasoning that they cannot have, or enjoy, a holiday because there is no one with whom to travel. There are, however, companies who set out to cater specifically for their needs. There are also holidays which are geared to a particular hobby and provide one with the opportunity to meet like-minded people. Whilst I recognise that travelling alone is not always easy, or ideal, we need to look at the attitude with which we approach it.

Making the most

A danger for the single person is being controlled by the thought of 'when I get married'. Some singles hold back from setting up their own home or making some major life decision because they want to wait until 'Mr/s Right' pops up. But what if he/she doesn't? *No marriage* is a possibility we all have to face at some stage. Peter Pan lived in Never-Never Land putting off growing up, and some singles lives in 'When-When Land, dreaming of 'the day'. I'm resident in When-When Land myself at times, but I'm learning that whilst the thoughts are captivating they rob me of present joy and opportunities.

Being on one's own, for many singles, means deprivation of certain comforts, sometimes even minor ones, because there is no one with whom to share these: 'If I were married I might indulge in that squidgy sofa' or 'If I were married I might bother to stock different teas'. Instead of 'indulging', the single person may adopt the mentality of 'getting by'. Is this right, or should we provide for ourselves in a way that we might do if we were married?

As singles, do we occasionally buy ourselves treats when we are 'low' in the way that we would for someone else? Do we give the same time and attention to cooking a meal for one as we do for two or more? Lack of money, often a reality, becomes an excuse for why people do not do for themselves what they would do for a partner. But there are ways around giving and being kind to oneself without being extravagant. For instance, not getting overstressed, taking time for relaxation and socialising, doing or buying oneself things which are not necessarily expensive but bring pleasure. For me this could mean having coffee with friends, a soak in a nicely scented bath, a mango from the market or going out for a nice meal.

Yes, there are problems and practicalities for the single person. But no, these do not have to be the battlefield we often make of them.

Part 2
Moving a mountain

5 | *Misconceptions*

Misconceptions about a person and his/her character can be very hurtful and damaging. Words which are sometimes spoken out of ignorance or lack of thought can so easily result in a person withdrawing or becoming defensive. It is like being stung by a scorpion each time a thoughtless word is spoken. Misconceptions regarding singleness can be indicated by direct or indirect words or actions, or by inference. The latter is often more difficult to confront. There is often also some confusion over what is inference by another and what is misinterpretation by the single person. It is easy to believe that you know what others think when, in reality, you have never actually found out what they think!

Bringing misconceptions to the surface is not a way of rubbing someone else's nose in the dirt. It is a way of bridging the gap in communication and understanding. Not all misconceptions are held by all married people yet it may be useful to raise some of the misconceptions which I have come across when talking to other singles. The following were all drawn from my singles questionnaire:

1. You have some major hang-up and therefore should be treated with suspicion and not permitted to participate in some forms of ministry.
2. You must be unbalanced, abnormal, strange, boring or gay otherwise you would have found a man/woman.
3. You lack a sense of responsibility – or you have no responsibilities.

4. You have failed in some way because you haven't achieved the 'norm' – status comes with marriage.
5. As a man you lack initiative and drive; as a woman you are too domineering or too weak.
6. You are inexperienced in life and unable to contribute much.
7. You can't maintain relationships or are frightened of commitment.
8. You are independent and therefore without need of affection.
9. You are career-minded, missionary-minded, or are not interested in marriage.
10. Because your marriage has broken up there must be some instability or lack of perseverance in you as a person.
11. You are lacking in charm, personality, intelligence, and are rather hard to fit into the pattern of life.
12. You are unfulfilled.
13. Coping is easy because you don't have a family to look after (even though some singles do!) therefore you have a lot of spare time.
14. If you seek contact with the opposite sex you are only after a partner.
15. You are not as capable in the practical aspects of life as those in couples.
16. You spend time in frivolous activities.
17. You need us to find you a partner.
18. You enjoy being alone.
19. It must be easier living alone without a partner to consider.
20. You don't look after yourself, i.e. don't cook properly.
21. Your identity needs to be linked to another individual (i.e. a partner).
22. You are always miserable about being single.
23. You are not fully mature, or you appear younger than you are.
24. You don't belong to anyone.

25. Singleness is a problem needing to be solved.
26. Singles only want to be with each other.

No doubt we could all add to this list with our own experiences of attitudes over the years. What strikes me as I talk with singles is that many of the misconceptions which arise from marrieds are inconsistent. As Linda Harding points out: 'The same Christians who would say that everyone is complete in Christ are often those who try to matchmake, or see single people as a problem, thus contradicting their own theology ... In the Church, a single man of thirty may be perceived as *going for God* while a single woman of the same age carries a feeling of *not having made it*'.[1]

Basically, the misconceptions all add up to one thing: 'something's not quite right with the single person!' Recently I attended an anger workshop for counsellors and trainee counsellors. At the end of the day we all had to say what we had gained. One of the trainee counsellors said: 'I used to think that I was a freak, now I realise that I am a freak amongst other freaks!' Maybe some marrieds think some singles are odd, maybe some singles think some marrieds are odd, but let's at least all *enjoy* being odd! Singles also hold misconceptions about marrieds. This brings us back to the importance of *communication* and *understanding*. If we want to move on and begin bridge-building instead of trench-digging we need to put these two principles into action a little more often.

Truth vs. unreality

How do misconceptions arise and how should singles challenge them? They arise through ignorance or failure to put oneself in someone else's shoes. To challenge a misconception we need first to identify it. Many singles live in a blur of painful existence and cannot put their finger on the root of the pain other than the fact that they are not married. One thing I learned about my own discovery of, and attempt at recovery from, painful events in the past was that *I had to work things out for myself*. Life is like a crossword puzzle: you can't move on until you've worked out the previous clue. You might dart around and try a completely different part of the puzzle but the fact remains that it will never be complete until all the clues are fathomed! We need to identify the misconceptions and look at how they are affecting us as individuals, and then we can formulate ways in which we can correct them. We have to bring the issues out into the open so that those who are 'guilty' of the misconceptions can understand singles and hopefully change their attitudes.

Let's take a brief look, from a broader perspective, at the misconceptions I listed earlier.

You have some major hang-up and therefore should be treated with suspicion and not permitted to participate in some forms of ministry. The idea that singleness should be equated with something 'not being right' is ridiculous. There are many single people who are 'together', gifted and capable. There are also single people who do have hang-ups and may not be able to cope with marriage, just as there are couples who have hang-ups and enter into marriage due to emotional dependency or escapism. Why should one's emotional stability and suitability for roles be measured in terms of marital status? Each person needs to be treated as an individual and assessed according to his/her suitability for certain roles. Being viewed with suspicion leaves the single person feeling that trust, earned in other circumstances, is being unfairly withheld.

You must be unbalanced, abnormal, strange, boring or gay otherwise you would have found a man/woman. Finding a man/woman is no indication that someone is not all these things anyway! Some singles have no desire to marry and it has nothing to do with emotional upset or sexual orientation. They are *happy* being single! Others want to marry but have not yet found, and may never find, someone. Some are more particular about what they want in a partner; others find their lifestyle limits their meeting many suitable people. As Christians, I think we also have to bear in mind the sovereignty of God. Can we say on the one hand that he is sovereign and has a plan for each of our lives, and on the other hand criticise the person who may be in God's will of 'no marriage at the moment'?

You lack a sense of responsibility – or you have no responsibilities. Why is it said that the single life has fewer responsibilities than the married? The single person who has never married or has no children does not have the same responsibilities as those who are married. Nevertheless, they still *have* responsibilities. Being a doctor, counsellor, teacher, or owning a home, or looking after aged parents are all situations of responsibility. Because the single person may seem to have more time to socialise with a variety of people, and may not have children to take care of, it does not mean that he/she does not have responsibilities or indeed is irresponsible.

You have failed in some way because you haven't achieved the 'norm' – status comes with marriage. Only until we stop seeing marriage as the 'norm' and begin to see marriage and singleness as equal choices will we lose this misconception. Questions such as 'Haven't you found someone yet?' create the belief that singleness is second best. There is constant pressure from society to date, as soon as you are old enough, and then to move towards marriage. People can so easily believe that happiness is primarily found in the fulfilment of marriage. Not having found someone is considered to be the individual's own fault with the suggestion that 'you can get married *if you want to*'. We all know that it's really not that simple.

Marriage is often seen as some wonderful transformer whereby a person shoots up the 'acceptance scale' overnight. Sometimes this is allied to the maturity issue, and sometimes it's more to do with achieving the 'norm' which some in society expect. These images can only change as people's attitudes change. Both marrieds and singles must be prepared to be more open and realistic about their struggles in life. We all need to begin to see people as people, not 'marrieds' and 'singles'.

As a man you lack initiative and drive; as a woman you are too domineering or too weak. There exists a mental image of unmarried Christian men as being like pieces of soggy lettuce. It's true that the church, at times, has had the tendency to attract people who are needy or struggle to fit in, but this is as true of couples as it is of singles.

Another criticism is that the Christian single woman can be too domineering. I think the submissive issue is often taken out of context and held over a woman who, through necessity of survival, has learned to look after herself. Being independent is sometimes interpreted as being domineering. I have no desire to be dominant but I'm not going to sit around waiting for someone else to speak when I have the answer on my tongue! This has occasionally been interpreted as being dominant. Other women are 'written off' because they are seen as weak and emotionally dependent. In some circumstances it is hard to know how one is 'supposed' to be and thereby avoid critical comment! The expectations of others often leave people unable to 'be themselves'.

You are inexperienced in life and unable to contribute much. People vary in their experiences, and some of us single folk have 'seen life' in various forms. Although still relatively young I have experienced many things, heard the most horrendous accounts of people damaged in childhood and adulthood, and I have been through trauma of various kinds from an early age myself. I have been with people who seriously self-harm and who have attempted suicide; I've lost friends through suicide and murder; I've seen poverty, leprosy, TB, polio; seen a child and an adult dying of cancer. I have seen richness, greed and self-centredness. I have known what it is to have and not to have. I have been criticised and misrepresented in public, and have been placed on a pedestal. I have slept in comfort and out in the open (on a mountain in Africa where there were leopards roaming). And I have eaten wildebeest sausages! I have been to a garden party at Lambeth Palace and I have sat with tramps. I have also contributed what I can to help some of the physical, emotional and spiritual decay in the world through work, understanding, travel, writing, counselling and financial giving. I am sure that many other singles have also truly 'seen life'. Experience is what we make of it; it is about our willingness to learn, to absorb life and to put ourselves out. It has nothing to do with marital status. Because single people are often perceived as sexually inexperienced they are sometimes also perceived as inexperienced in life.

You can't maintain relationships or are frightened of commitment. Some singles would agree with this and would benefit from help, whilst most would long for the chance of long-term relationships and commitment. Just because a person is not in a relationship does not mean that he/she cannot handle one. Those who are unable to maintain relationships or who are frightened of commitment are more in need of help than of being pushed aside as odd.

You are independent and therefore without need of affection. Independence has somehow been equated with all-round self-sufficiency, with an 'I can cope on my own and have no need of other's mentality'. To develop a level of self-sufficiency in order to handle the practicalities of life does not mean that one is without emotional needs. Perhaps some people need to learn to let go of the belief that admitting to needs is a sign of weakness. This is not just an issue faced by singles.

You are career-minded, missionary-minded, or are not interested in marriage. Not all, in fact very few, singles feel 'called' to be single and so want to devote their lives only to other purposes. Sometimes there is a conflict between career/ministry and marriage, and the single person is left feeling he/she wants both to maintain work and to find fulfilment in marriage and having a family. Such a combination is not unusual and it is good for the single person to air any such ambivalence and desires.

Because your marriage has broken up there must be some instability or lack of perseverance in you as a person. Why, when a relationship breaks up, do people make an assumption that the parties are people who 'give up' or that one of them, at least, has a 'character defect'? There are so many reasons why a marriage or relationship does not continue. One woman told me about the physical and emotional abuse she and her children had endured within her marriage. Her husband was a minister and she felt very alone. After endless futile suggestions from her that they should seek help, she finally left. Can you blame her? Would it have been right for her to stay married, and to put her children through further abuse, just so that she would not been seen as someone who lacked stability? We should all be wary of jumping to unfounded conclusions in such matters.

You are lacking in charm, personality, intelligence, and are rather hard to fit into the pattern of life. It's strange how marriage seems to be equated with the positive aspects of personality whilst singleness is often equated with the negative. When I lecture on compulsive eating I talk about the media inference which links certain criteria with being slim: being in control, happier, sophisticated, successful, respected, liked, sexually attractive, feminine, wanted. Do we honestly believe that anyone who is overweight is unable to have these qualities? This same 'criteria mentality' sometimes applies to the way marrieds and singles are viewed: as soon as you marry you attain certain qualities! The most obvious of which is moving from a position of inexperience, immaturity and instability to a position of experience, maturity and stability. The very words often related to marriage 'settled down' suggest an element of irresponsibility within the single.

You are unfulfilled. As a single person you might be unfulfilled, in the sense that there may be a part of your needs which are not *fully* met. But it does not mean that you have to go without fulfilment in the wider context. Life as a single person can be extremely fulfilling and it can help if other people see and understand this.

Coping is easy because you don't have a family to look after (even though some singles do!) therefore you have a lot of spare time. Most singles don't have a family to care for, and for many of these people life *is* relatively easy. Yet so much depends on the specifics in each individual's life. We need to be careful not to generalise. Some single people lead very busy lives and have demanding jobs – both in terms of time and emotions. The amount of stress each person can handle also needs to be taken into consideration. We all have different tolerance levels, and some may feel the support of a family actually helps to relieve their difficulties and stress.

Single people without children may have more 'spare time', in the sense of being freer to choose what they do with their time. They may have greater flexibility. But in terms of daily chores, these may be similar for couples and singles. Single people still have to cook, wash up, iron, clean, shop, do the gardening, answer the post, see to the car, etc. The chores aren't halved and are often on top of a hard day's work. A single mother, who works during the day, recalled how she dragged herself out of bed when suffering from flu: 'The water tank was leaking, the heating was off and I'd got no money to put things right,' she said. 'I still had to cook and clear up – there was no one else to do it.'

If you seek contact with the opposite sex you are only after a partner. A single person's perceived 'desperation' for marriage can give this impression, which can be off-putting to the opposite sex and even to friends. Whilst there may be an element of truth in the desperation theory, if people take time to talk to singles they will find that most would not want a marriage which fell to pieces. In the majority of cases, marriage for the sake of marriage is not the goal, and therefore contact with the opposite sex can be for the sake of friendship not just relationship. I like Susan Page's motto for the single person: 'Determination without Depression'.[2]

You are not as capable in the practical aspects of life as those in couples. This is a bit like saying 'How long is a piece of string?' We cannot put all singles into the same box. Perhaps more couples should ask singles to give them a hand with the DIY. Anyway, are *all* married people capable?

You spend time in frivolous activities. Some singles do, some don't, and some of us wish we could! The single's socialising can be seen as frivolous by some married people. Yet what is frivolous to one person may be of great importance to another. I rarely have time to waste on frivolous activities. When I was working long hours, writing a book, doing my regular job, *and* answering the dozens of letters I receive I used to feel that many married people were fortunate to have cosy Sunday afternoons at home and evenings of unwinding after the kids were in bed. I probably misunderstood them as much as others have misunderstood me at times. The grass is always greener on the other side.

You need us to find you a partner. The number of times married people try to matchmake can be infuriating to single people! People keeping their 'eyes open' for you can be a compliment, but at other times it hurts. After my broken engagement I could not cope with the thought of meeting another man and I needed people to be sensitive about this. The mention of a suitable person having been spotted, which in the past would have raised my hopes, only caused deep pain. Some singles have never been interested in marriage and have no intention of changing their situation. For them, matchmaking or the assumption that they have such an interest in marriage is difficult.

You enjoy being alone. Because the single person might be put in the position of spending a great deal of time alone, it does not mean that he/she enjoys being alone. It is also easy to make the assumption that if the person doesn't enjoy being alone then they should just find someone to be with. There are many singles who don't enjoy being alone but, at the same time, who struggle to make friends or find asking for support or company difficult. These people often wait to be asked to join others, and others fail to recognise their need. So, the lonely become more lonely and the outgoing go out more and more often.

It must be easier living alone without a partner to consider. Certainly in living alone there is more potential for self-centredness. But, although singles do not have a partner to consider, not all singles live alone. Sharing a house or looking after an aged parent also means considering other people's needs. I wouldn't say that not having a partner is easier - it's simply different.

You don't look after yourself, i.e. don't cook properly. There is the temptation for many singles not to take as much care over food, although some eat just as well. When I lived alone I ate as healthily as I would have done if I had been married, but possibly I did not introduce as much variety as I would have done if I had been preparing for two. One area where singles often fall short when solo catering is in the presentation of food. When was the last time a married couple ate out of a pan standing at the cooker? This is not uncommon for singles!

I have often found that married people give single people little bits of food when they have visited for the day. I think it is kind and I always receive it with gratitude, but occasionally the manner in which this is done can leave the single person feeling a bit like a charity case. It is important for single people to entertain couples (where possible) so that the giving is equal. Not returning a couple's hospitality can end up with the single person feeling that he/she is a victim and the couple feeling that they are mere meal providers.

Your identity needs to be linked to another individual (i.e. a partner). Identity is so often indicated by who you 'belong to': 'This is so-and-so's wife'; 'Meet my husband'; 'Oh, who are you with?' The single person can be left with the question 'Who am I?' He/she has to find an alternative indicator for identity. One's profession is usually an acceptable substitute, but does it stimulate the same feelings of belonging? I believe that establishing a strong sense of identity in one's own right is important for both singles and couples. Each of us can answer the question 'Who am I?' in its most basic form: 'I am a child of God, made in his image'. Therefore, there is a part of our identity we can develop: becoming more like God in character.

Then there are other factors which figure; factors which make us unique. These include our likes, dislikes and character qualities. Each day I discover more about myself: some aspects I may want to change and some to develop. These areas of my identity are not directly linked to another individual. A part of our identity, especially in marriage, *is* linked to another person, but not in a binding way which kills individuality. We do not need another person to enable us to have a strong sense of identity; we need to know and be confident in ourselves.

You are always miserable about being single. For most singles who want to get married there are nearly always moments when one is miserable about being single. Or perhaps a better word is saddened. But onlookers need to see that these are moments amongst other moments. I had such a moment recently. I looked at a newly-married couple's wedding photographs and started thinking about my own unused wedding dress stored in its cardboard box. Then a married friend phoned and told me that she was pregnant. I ached for marriage and for a family. The next morning I tried to remember that there were, and are, other rewarding aspects to life. The satisfaction I find in creative and artistic pursuits releases my hurts. Some people *do* appear miserable all the time about their state of singleness. Maybe they need to be helped to develop others aspects of their lives which can bring satisfaction and fulfilment.

You are not fully mature, or you appear younger than you are. I mentioned earlier how singles are often seen as not yet mature. Clive, in his late forties, said: 'In my experience singles are frequently ignored and not considered in decision-making. The inference is that everyone is either married or is still a child.' Until people are able to see maturity for what it is this misconception will remain. As singles, we need to speak about and work towards maturity in its entirety. What does this involve?

- accepting responsibility for ourselves
- being willing to face and feel our emotions
- being willing to work on our problems
- being committed to personal growth
- having faith and trust in God
- asking for help when needed
- loving others without judgement
- seeing the world through other people's eyes
- being able to make choices
- knowing our needs
- having a healthy means of meeting our needs
- having good self-esteem, yet remaining humble
- having purpose and direction in life
- being in a state of continual learning about life
- allowing pain to be a tool for growth
- being free to be oneself

All of these are possible whether we are single or married.

You don't belong to anyone. This misconception can be very painful, as we all need a sense of belonging. Usually the single person interprets this need as only belonging to one special or particular person. As with the misconception concerning maturity, we need to redefine 'belonging'. We do not have to belong to *a person* in order to feel that we belong. As singles, it is true that we do not have a lifetime partner and so do not experience belonging in this sense. But we can find belonging in our faith, our friendships and our interests, and this requires personal involvement and commitment. It is, at least in part, up to us when we walk into church, or some other gathering, whether we have a strong sense of belonging or not.

Singleness is a problem needing to be solved. This is probably the greatest misunderstanding, for as long as singleness is seen as a problem, singles will be seen as people with problems. We don't talk about the *problem* of children, we talk about the *needs* of children. To meet their needs in a church setting, a crèche, Sunday School and often other activities exist. The needs of children change and hopefully the children's programme is constantly reviewed. When children have specific needs these are dealt with, inside or outside the church. We must start to talk about the *needs* of singles and look at ways in which we could meet those needs. Yet, if we define singles purely as a group who are in need of support, we categorise them as people who need only to receive and are incapable of giving. Singles should be treated as people who happen to be single and are capable of giving as well as of receiving.

Singles only want to be with each other. Singles probably think the same of couples! Many singles spend time together mainly because they are available at the same times. The single person's greatest time of need for socialising is often in the evening, which is also the loneliest time. This is the very moment when people with children are usually busiest. Rather than making assumptions about how either singles or couples like to spend time, let's be honest and open enough to ask.

How do single people feel as a result of all the unspoken and spoken misconceptions? No doubt some feel 'invisible', 'unimportant', overlooked'. Whilst singleness is not a problem to be solved, the attitude towards and the handling of the issue of singleness within the Church *is* a problem. A problem exists only when it is defined as such, and so it is important that if singles feel misrepresented they say so.

One church which contacted me conducted an evening of looking at singleness issues. They sent me this list of points which were made:

1. Most people did not agree with Paul's statement in 1 Corinthians that it is better to remain single. (Had they received fuller teaching about the circumstances lying behind this they might have seen it somewhat differently.)
2. Most people felt the Church viewed single people differently from married people. They are considered as having a great deal of free time and are therefore asked to be involved in numerous church activities and end up burning themselves out. This also means that they have little spare time to meet people of their own age and that they are always giving rather than receiving.
3. In many churches there is a preponderance of females, so the issues related to singleness appeared greater for the women in the group.
4. For men there isn't the same urgency to marry – the thirties seem a more reasonable option. Women tend to feel that time is running out concerning child-bearing.
5. The words used to describe the singleness of men and women conjure up different images. 'Bachelor' sounds like a man who has chosen to remain young, free and single; whereas 'spinster' sounds old, frumpy, and people tend to associate it with 'being left on the shelf'.
6. Most people considered themselves to be in an interim state rather than being 'called' to be single.

7. Church sermons are mainly concerned with married couples and families; few concentrate on being single.
8. Many people said that they felt lonely, lacking the support of a partner, and were not happy with their situation.
9. The group agreed that there are a large number of single people both within the Church and outside, whose problems the Church did not seem to be addressing. With one in eight Christian marriages breaking up, it was thought of as a subject which the Church should certainly not ignore.

The discussion led this particular group to consider practical ways of dealing with singleness. These were:

- Get to know families within the church – there can be mutual support. This also means the single person is not always surrounded by other single people. This can be achieved not only by accepting hospitality but also by giving it.
- Once a week make an effort to go out and take part in some kind of social activity with someone else.
- Have a prayer partner. This will enable you to share things and be honest.
- Be positive and make the most of the situation God has allowed you to be in.

Often change in the attitude towards singles, and the treatment of them, does not occur because those in leadership positions don't realise that anything is wrong. I would encourage singles who feel that they are being treated differently because they are single, or who feel uncomfortable with misconceptions and attitudes, not to wait for things to change but to be the instigators of change.

6 | Stumbling Blocks

In the last chapter I suggested that the Church cannot understand or change if singles do not speak up. As well as singles speaking up the Church needs to be willing to look at its attitudes and practices which might be a stumbling block for the single person. Romans 14:13 says: *Therefore let us not judge one another anymore, but rather determine this – not to put an obstacle or stumbling block in a brother's way.* (NASB) The Greek word for stumbling block is *skandalon,* which also means offence. 'In the New Testament *skandalon* is always used metaphorically, and ordinarily of anything that arouses prejudice, or becomes a hindrance to others, or causes them to fall by the way.'[1] The Church's attitude towards the single person can, on occasions, be described as having been prejudiced, having been a hindrance to some and having resulted in a few people falling by the way. 'The essence of equality or inequality is not so much the *treatment* we give people as the *value* we put on them. The former is only, after all, an expression of the latter.'[2]

'Marrieds/Singles divide'

The greatest stumbling block in the Church regarding singleness is the 'marrieds / singles divide': the fact that a clear distinction is made between the two states, and that singles are not seen or treated in the same way as marrieds. Julia Duin points out that 'the Church is the only institution which separates people into groups of marrieds and singles – people who have and people who have not.'[3] The Church so often seems to want to see single people married, as though they are not complete until this happens and the service they give is not 'full service' until they have 'settled down'. These, and other attitudes, can be very damaging. By way of example, the following woman's experience would have been sufficient to put some people off the Church altogether:

> In 1992 I attended a prayer conference at a local church. The speaker read Jesus' words in Matthew 18:19: *Again, I tell you that if two of you on earth agree about anything you ask for, it will be done for you by my Father in heaven.* My brother and I had, on many occasions, stood on this word concerning events in our family. But the speaker started to interpret it as though it was particularly designed for married couples. As the talk progressed my overall impression was that God didn't really listen to you unless you were married and that he highly favoured married couples. After a while I began to feel that perhaps the problem was in me as, by this stage, I was not enjoying the talk.
>
> The talk ended with a call for single people to stand at the front of the congregation. My hopes rose as I thought that this seemingly insensitive man had become slightly more sensitive. Perhaps he was going to pray for us all to be blessed with partners or for healing for past damaged relationships. But no, this was not to be. What followed was what, to me, felt like the ultimate intimidation. The singles had been set aside, told to bow our heads and *not* to look at the married couples. The speaker then prayed for the married couples, asked God to bless them and asked them to pray for each other. I felt as if I might as well have been standing on the street naked: having been brought to the front for nothing. I felt exposed, awkward and foolish. I was enraged at the insensitivity of this man towards all the single people who trustingly went forward at his command.

> By this stage I was hurting deeply and near to tears. A married lady, seeing my distress but not finding out the cause of it, came up to me and said, *The Lord is your husband*. The words come from Isaiah 54:5 and are spoken to Israel, relating God as a husband to the *whole* Church, not specifically to the single person. Her 'speaking into my situation' only added to my distress.
>
> Time has passed and the wounds have healed but I still pray that the speaker becomes more sensitive to those who, often through circumstance, find themselves in a single state and struggle with it. Society seems more understanding and more gracious than the Church, which is sad when you consider that the Church is supposed to be a caring place.

It is not just the 'marrieds/singles divide' which presents problems but the fact that marriage is seen as a yardstick for measuring many things. Those who have 'not yet partaken' are at the bottom of the scale, whilst those who have 'achieved it' are at the top. Engaged couples are on their way up, whilst a broken engagement or divorce is like falling off altogether! It seems that there are different interpretations by those of us who have yet to 'make the grade', depending upon our situation and favour. We are viewed as one of the following:

- potentially there (have everything that it takes and someone in mind)
- waiting for it to happen (have some of what it takes but no takers)
- miles off (have nothing of what it takes and definitely no takers)
- having tried and failed (possibly had what it takes but 'goofed')

If marriage is the 'ultimate', is singleness the 'pits'? It seems that we live in a world of extreme thinking and ridiculous rating! Anne, a woman in her mid-fifties, said that in her church whenever the vicar reads the banns for a couple who are to marry, he often says that marriage is God's plan for us and prays as though it is the only option chosen by sensible people. This could be because he doesn't want couples co-habiting but could also be an indictment against singles.

The way in which some people react to singles can be condescending or patronising; through pity, single people can feel that they are objects of sympathy. Glib comments can be unhelpful and hurtful. We all say things which wound others and often it results from a lack of really understanding the other person's position. Sometimes comments which are made to singles, specifically about their state, are said with the best of intentions but result in great irritation. Here are some true, if somewhat sardonic, examples of the gap in thinking between the married and single person:

Married says: 'You'll be the next up the aisle.'
Single thinks: 'Oh yeah! Where's the evidence?'

Married says: 'Why don't you get married?'
Single thinks: 'Because finding a partner is a little more complex that buying a chicken.'

Married says: 'Anyone on the horizon?'
Single thinks: 'Wait a minute; I'll just get out the binoculars!'

Married says: 'What you need is a man/woman.'
Single thinks: 'Find me one!'

If only people were more sensitive! An unhelpful mentality is the *when* mentality. Questions are often asked of singles: 'When are you going to settle down?' 'When are you going to find someone?' The little word *if* doesn't seem to enter the picture. As singles, should we let these comments pass us by or should we be more honest? 'Thank you for being concerned, but I really struggle with what you have just said as I find it fills me with false hope.' It is not that what is said is necessarily wrong or inaccurate, although sometimes it is not based on fact. But even if it is true, so often there is a lack of sensitivity in the way in which things are presented.

Perhaps it is difficult for those who have been married for many years to remember what the 'single existence' was like. For those who have never experienced long periods on their own there is little concept of what singleness is about. People say 'We've all been single' but some people literally moved from their parents' home (and virtual adolescence) to marriage, and have no idea! Even so, this should be no excuse for not trying to empathise. We do not have to have the same experiences as the person we are endeavouring to understand in order to have empathy. If we did, we would live our life from crisis to crisis. Yet, surely one part of being a Christian is all about empathy and 'getting alongside'.

One of the most damaging of experiences, however, is when a Christian person uses 'prophecy' (without truly hearing from God) as a means of expressing their hope for the single person. Once, a woman I knew received a 'prophecy' that I would marry and have three children. She had seen a picture of the man I was to marry and the first child I was to have. A short while later I started dating a guy and, when the woman met him, she confirmed that this was the man she had seen in her dream. As the relationship progressed things became extremely uncomfortable as I discovered unconfessed ongoing sexual sin/addiction in his life, but I kept saying to God: 'If this really is the man then I will love him.' Eventually I realised that the whole 'prophecy' was wrong and I broke off the relationship. I was accused by the man of 'being a strong-willed woman who went against the will of God'. Later, I realised that prophecy is to *confirm* what God has already placed on our heart, not to be used like fortune-telling. I know that my situation is not unique and that it is not unusual for prophecy or words of knowledge to be misused when interpreting issues connected with relationship and marriage. Such 'words of knowledge' frequently leave the single person feeling frustrated, angry, alone, embarrassed, empty and, in some cases, doubting that he/she can hear God.

Another comment often made by singles is that they very rarely hear a sermon on singleness or even with singleness used as an example. This is in contrast to the number of marriage illustrations. Situations as simple as this strengthen the belief within the single that he/she is of less significance than the married person.

Sadly, it is not just the single *person* who is ostracised but the single *woman*. To be single and to be a woman, in some circles, is a double negative. It means bias, fewer opportunities and subservience. Is that the way Jesus treated women? A non-Christian friend was sharp to point out to me, as I recalled how I was treated on one occasion within a church: 'That isn't the way I see Jesus.' There is a vast need for change within the Church if we are not to be seen by outsiders as hypocrites. Beth felt moved to speak out in church, which is not unusual in some of the 'freer' services. Still seated she spoke quietly: *God is within us* (1 John 4:15). 'With these words,' she said, 'I was forcibly ejected from the congregation and made to feel like a heretic … I feel pretty sure that had I been sitting next to a man, had I been a part of a couple, this would not have happened.'

Why does the Church so often treat marrieds and singles differently? Many churches are largely made up of middle class professional people. The 'norm' for such people is a progressive state: being a student (single and immature); then starting a career (married and maturing); finally, being established in a career (family and maturity).

Anyone who doesn't fit into this pattern is in a 'no-man's land': not a student, yet not seen as being mature.

Churches often pride themselves in being 'family friendly', and it would appear that there is greater sensitivity to the needs and pressures on married people. Maybe this is because most church leaders are married and relate more easily to married people. Usually, if one partner is under stress, ill or going through some trial, the other partner can inform the church. If a single person is going through such a trial and feeling emotionally crippled it may mean that he / she finds it too hard to ask for support and that no one is doing the asking on his / her behalf. Adam was severely depressed and felt suicidal. 'I had a five-minute chat with one of the elders and that was about the sum total of pastoral care that I received. A few months ago one of the deacons in my church (who is married) was depressed to the point of being off work for several weeks. His family received much practical support and several people took time to pray with him.'

Many singles find that the services and the facilities within the church are targeted at families. This leaves the single person feeling like an 'oddity', as Cora describes: 'Because churches are frequently family-oriented it makes one feel that being single is wrong.' Even the illustration of the Church being a family is off-putting to some singles, who feel very sensitive to the family concept or who long for their own family and feel on the fringe of other people's. Other singles find the concept of belonging to a 'family' group helpful.

Another stumbling block is the attitude of some towards the divorced person. There are people who carry a negative, even condescending, attitude towards anyone who has been caught up in a broken marriage. Yet the divorced person may often be in great pain. John Littlewood, a pastor, puts this into perspective:

> The circumstances of divorce are seldom easy, nor can they be made pleasant. Our law courts employ an adversarial way of dealing with divorce. In a short time one partner moves from being surrounded by others to being on their own in a strange home. This is seldom recognised or sympathised with. They experience symptoms akin to those of bereavement and need care from the church family.
>
> In many churches what they experience is condemnation. Sometimes I have worked with a couple for months and only after great agony and heart-searching is the decision sadly taken to divorce. Then insensitive people barge in with no knowledge of the situation, making judgements and pronouncements that deeply wound. 'Couldn't you have worked harder to keep the marriage together?' I wish that Christians would be as strong on charity as they are on judgement and would learn to pray into situations instead of declaring themselves as judge and jury. I wish that they would be as ready to come forward to serve a brother or sister who is hurting, even someone who is the cause of a marriage break-up. What they need is love and care; a practical out-working of the love of Christ. Jesus always loves first, even when faced with real sin, as the gospel accounts demonstrate.[4]

Sometimes the Church fosters a negative attitude towards singleness and the single person. Andrew Cornes, a vicar and the author of *Divorce and Remarriage*, commenting on Paul's words to the Corinthians, points out:

> Paul is not afraid to weigh up the respective merits of marriage and singleness; he is not shy of answering the question 'Which is better?' And he comes down unequivocally on the side of singleness ... this Chris-

tian view was revolutionary in its day, being almost unheard of in pagan or Jewish circles. It did, however, take hold of the minds and hearts of Christians who were convinced Paul was right, and the single life was highly honoured and respected in the early Church, sometimes even going beyond the teaching of St Paul. Today this teaching is almost totally unheard, at least in Protestant circles. Who would dare to say that singleness is better than marriage? On the contrary, the unspoken – and often spoken – assumption of almost everyone is that marriage is better than singleness. Yet the apostle Paul says the reverse, and undergirds his statement with arguments which are just as valid today … as they were when he first wrote them.

Paul of course said specifically that while a man who marries his intended does well, *he who does not marry does better* (1 Corinthians 7:38), and although this is the clearest place in which he states that the single life is to be preferred to marriage, it is in fact clearly his position throughout the chapter…

Every Christian, and particularly every Christian contemplating marriage however far in the future it may be (1 Corinthians 7:36–38), should seek to come to terms with this New Testament teaching. It is true that marriage, not singleness, may well be "better" in our particular case (e.g. 1 Corinthians 7:9), but until we have come to see that singleness is at least as much a gift from God as marriage, and that for many people it is the better state, we have not come to see singleness and marriage through New Testament eyes.

This calls for understanding. To the contemporary Westerner it is extremely difficult to get our mind – still less our heart – round this idea that singleness is as good as, and even better than, marriage. Our whole upbringing and culture has shouted the contrary. Both Jesus and Paul recognised the problem. It is precisely what Jesus said: *Not everyone accepts* (not 'can accept' as in NIV) *this word* and why he exclaims at the end of his teaching on singleness: *Let him who can accept this accept it.* (Matthew 19:11, 12) ... The word used here is *choreo*. It means 'grasp in the mental sense, comprehend, understand'. It was to help his disciples understand why singleness is good that Jesus gave his teaching in Matthew 19:11f; it was to help the Christians at Corinth to understand why the single life is preferable that Paul argued it through in 1 Corinthians 7:25ff. And if we, in the late twentieth century, are to gain a true understanding of singleness in God's purposes we must pore over and seek to understand these crucial passages.

And that comes down to the Church: preaching on these passages, setting them for house-group Bible studies, having talks on them in church youth groups and student Christian groups, so that the New Testament's views on singleness become part of the world-view, and the self-understanding of ordinary Christians.[5]

Equal consideration

Within many churches there does not appear to be equal consideration when choosing someone for a ministry in the church: the single status may override a person's ability and sensibility. Some churches hold the view that being single disqualifies one from being a deacon, an elder or a house-group leader. Adam is a mature Christian, intelligent and very knowledgeable regarding biblical facts. He is in a church with an all-male and all-married leadership, yet was asked to be a house group leader. However, it was made quite clear that his position was *until* they found a 'suitable married couple'. It is no wonder that many singles feel 'not quite good enough', that unless they marry it is impossible to 'make the grade' in the eyes of church leaders. For single people to gain right worth they need to be allowed to assume positions of responsibility, to be treated as trustworthy, rather than having to prove themselves.

Linda Harding makes some interesting comments regarding why there are so few single church leaders:

> At the one extreme there is the Roman Catholic Church which has seen virginity for priests as the means of releasing time and energies into devotion to God, and therefore requires it for priesthood (this would appear to be based on Paul's exhortation to the Corinthian church to abstain from sex in order to devote themselves to prayer). At the other extreme, churches have interpreted literally Paul's advice to Timothy that leaders should be the husband of one wife. Somewhere in the middle others would see that single people are capable of limited leadership responsibility, i.e. they would not be able to teach, pastor or counsel on issues related to marriage or children. In fact their usefulness may be restricted to other singles of the same sex. This shows incredible prejudice, since no similar restriction is placed on married people teaching or counselling singles. Being single certainly did not restrict Jesus or Paul in their teaching on marriage, sexual ethics, etc. I do not believe the Bible says that a person's marital status affects their eligibility to lead in the Church.[6]

Perhaps the attitudes within a church stem from the top. If leaders do not set an example of treating singles as equals – with the same opportunities, abilities and even social invitations – how can they expect others to do likewise? There is a need to accept singles as equal but different, as people who have something to contribute, not as people who have missed out in some way.

A common remark by single women, in particular, is that they seem to be considered as only of use for the crèche and Sunday School. Some single women find this odd since they have less experience, and in some cases no experience, of dealing with children. Some women find that working with children is one way of sublimating their maternal instincts, whilst others find it particularly painful. Being placed in these roles, rather than being involved in services, can also result in them feeling excluded.

Sometimes there is a failure to distinguish between personal beliefs (about what is right and wrong) and the individual as a person. Everyone has their own beliefs, for instance, about divorce and remarriage. But the view of a concept should not be entangled with the view of the person. In some churches single parents continue to feel as if they are treated as outcasts or as though they are people lacking something. There can also be, especially for a woman, repression of freedom of speech and spontaneity.

The Church doesn't always think to include singles unless they are assertive or very gifted. People's attitudes towards a person are so often connected with the status of the individual. I find that I am treated differently now, with my name in print and being known in certain counselling and speaking circles, than I was before I achieved public recognition. I am treated with much greater respect and taken far more seriously. There seems to be a status ladder for singles. As a well-known, intelligent, articulate and educated single who loves people I receive far more invitations and 'attention' than many single people I have known. The person who is shy, less educated, less articulate and maybe has some irritating mannerisms is often left out. But is this right? Shouldn't we be treating each other with the same regard, and be prepared to give each other the same amount of time?

Finally, when I asked one woman in what ways she felt the Church falls short, her reply was 'Not evangelising all those single men "out there"!' I think the majority of single women would should a loud 'Amen'.

Many men seem to feel that they don't need church. They see church as a feminine place, with its emphasis on feelings. Some single men are uncomfortable with the obvious imbalance of more women than men, whilst other men do not want to be hypocritical regarding their sexual drive. How can the Church encourage men to be more involved? This is one area which should concern the whole congregation, not just single women.

Change and responsibility

Much of what I have said in this chapter could be misconstrued as condemning the Church. My intention is rather that it should be seen as constructive criticism, and that its most important outcome be change.

The bottom line is that the Church needs to provide a positive reinforcement for singleness. Singleness is rarely, if ever, presented as a fulfilling option. When it has been presented thus it is in the context of being 'called to serve'. Yet many singles argue that they don't feel 'called' and reason that they could serve better if they had the moral support of a loving partner. For those who have been 'called' there can be negative attitudes which lead to stress, as Kim explains: 'The external difficulties are mainly having my "calling" misunderstood or not accepted, and having few others in this state with whom to identify.'

One young man wrote a report to his church leaders about singleness. I found the following points particularly interesting:

- The word 'single' is a catch-all term that assumes that a single professional male in his late twenties faces the same challenges and problems as an elderly widow.
- Singles often perceive 'single' as meaning 'one who has failed to find a mate'. They may resent being labelled 'a failure'. Any help given to single people must be given with the utmost tact and sensitivity.

- The term 'single' risks polarising the Church between single and married people. Ultimately, the term is a dehumanising one. Being single is *one* attribute of a person's life, not the totality of it.

For the single person caught up in a system where singles are treated differently, it can feel as though nothing will change.

In contrast, it is refreshing when one hears of a church where there is a broad outlook on singles – where singles are included, given the same opportunities and are not treated differently. Sue has found this to be so in her church: 'I am fortunate in my church that being single and a woman does not bar me from leadership. Other churches take a different stance on this. My spare time is not presumed upon; I am free to choose my duties.'

When talking about whether the Church has helped, Karen, another single woman, said: 'I would not say the "Church" as an entity has helped. My faith has helped, as I know I've always got God to talk to, and my friends within the church have been sympathetic and more encouraging than non-Christian friends in the same circumstances.' Perhaps this should leave us thinking a little more deeply about where the responsibility for our happiness as singles lies. Whilst it is the responsibility of the Church to cater for everyone equally, is it the Church's or the individual's responsibility to enable singleness to be a positive experience? Surely both have a part to play.

7 | *Inner attitudes*

There's a little verse which goes: 'Two men looked out from prison bars. One saw mud, one saw stars.' The choice to see singleness as a problem or as an opportunity is that of the individual. It is so easy when we are asked questions about our single state to feel self-conscious or even guilty for *still* being single. For women, the first thing friends we haven't seen for some time often ask us is: 'Have you found someone yet?' Usually the single person is left feeling a sense of failure or disappointment. Poor self-esteem concerning our state is often based on incorrect thinking. An old adage says: 'We are not what we think we are; we are not what others think we are; we are what we think others think we are.' Only the single person's positive attitude towards singleness will change other people's negative attitudes. In other words, change begins with us. What's important is not what we are now, but what we are willing to become. Cliff Richard was once asked by a publisher to write about the *problem* of singleness. As he began to write, he realised that it wasn't a problem! Cliff's handling of media hounding over why he is single also offers a positive example:

> For me, being single isn't a drag or a pressure. It doesn't cause dark depression or make me lie awake bemoaning what might have been. I really doubt if I'm a bundle of sexual hang-ups and frustrations. In a nutshell, I actually enjoy being single!
>
> How many times have I kicked myself for falling into the trap of defending the fact that I'm single?

> You've heard the question, with the not-so-subtle innuendo, "Why haven't you married then?" Maybe single people should start reversing the tables. "Why on earth did you get married?" That would flummox a few!
>
> Then there's the other equally-irritating approach: "Haven't you ever thought about settling down?" The fact is that I'm probably vastly more "settled down" than the questioner … It's amazing how so many people's minds just can't grasp that the single man or woman isn't necessarily inadequate, gay or abnormal, and that it's actually possible to pursue a single lifestyle perfectly happily, healthily, and without experiencing appalling deprivation.[1]

People have different attitudes towards their singleness and may view it in the light of other factors influencing their lives, especially unresolved hurts. In Chapter 5 we looked at misconceptions other people may have regarding singleness. Unfortunately, single people sometimes come to conclusions about themselves, based on these misconceptions, which are inaccurate or damaging to self-esteem. A few people I have met have had such a low opinion of themselves that even though they desire marriage they feel they don't deserve it. If we do not have positive feelings about ourselves and our single state then outsiders' attitudes will accentuate the bad feelings we already have, resulting in the experience becoming unbearable. It is upon reaching such a point that some singles have had breakdowns.

Though the attitudes of others are painful and can be very destructive, our internal attitudes are possibly more destructive because we carry them around with us each day. They can become like a knife twisting and grinding in our tender bodies. Though we carry our attitudes around with us, we have a choice as to the extent of the pain we feel. It is not so much our circumstances which result in painful feelings but our interpretation of those circumstances. This is a concept which can help us enormously, shifting us from a despised singleness which is a constant state of agony to limited pain and deep growth. (I explore the concept of thinking affecting feelings in greater detail in my book *Beyond Chaotic Eating*.)

Childhood experiences

Childhood experiences, positive and negative, can affect the way we perceive and cope with life and hence with singleness. In my research for this book quite a number of the people questioned reported difficulties in their home background, which they felt could have contributed towards their struggles with singleness and with forming lasting relationships. Here are some of the people who shared their experiences:

Steve is in his mid-forties. He remembers being an unwanted and unloved child with a violent, alcoholic father. Withdrawal and isolation contributed to his finding friendships (especially with the opposite sex) very difficult. Homosexuality became a pattern as he wrestled with ambivalent feelings of love and hate towards his father. He realises, now, that through his interaction with other men he may even have been trying to recreate the father relationship; wanting to find a different ending to the sad story of his childhood. He has subsequently moved away from the homosexual life.

Tom is in his early thirties and had an authoritarian and unaffectionate mother. He had one brother and no sisters, and there was little contact with any other children. Soon after his brother was born his parents stopped sleeping together. Tom also went to a single-sex boarding school where he had a strict, uncompassionate housemother. He now struggles with finding any comfort in a woman's femininity.

Barbara is in her early forties and is divorced. She had a very disruptive childhood, with parents who constantly argued. Her parents stayed together until Barbara was twenty-one, at which point her father walked out. She remembers her younger years as desperately unhappy. She now sees that her childhood experience failed to provide a good role-model for marriage and family life, and she feels that it may have been a factor in her choice of a partner and consequent divorce.

Louise is in her mid-twenties and had a strict upbringing. There was no freedom to talk about issues such as sexuality and no expression of affection between her parents in front of her sister or herself. Her father found it difficult to talk about his, or other people's, feelings and her mother was very anxious and controlling. As she looks back on her childhood she would describe her life as having been dominated by fear and guilt. She finds relating to other people difficult, feels lonely, constantly tries to please others, has little self-esteem, and at times struggles with self-destructive thoughts.

There are many childhood experiences which can affect a person's ability to relate, form friendships, and be relaxed with the opposite sex. Often we don't realise how underlying fears, hurts and anxieties – and consequent behaviour patterns – may have influenced our inability to form stable, lasting relationships, or why we find singleness so painful. Some childhood experiences which may be influential in adulthood are:

- divorce or death of parent(s)
- parents who had a turbulent relationship
- bullying or severe teasing
- single-sex school or boarding school
- no siblings or friends of the opposite sex
- sexual, emotional or physical abuse
- overly controlled environment

The list of situations is endless. Whilst we cannot take time back, we can look at the issues in our lives which have contributed to the problems and resolve to work at change. It is at this stage that counselling may be helpful. Many churches offer marriage preparation counselling, but what many people need is *relationship* preparation counselling. We need to sort out the problems before they get carried into a marriage. Many relationships and marriages fail due to emotional pain and behavioural patterns which have never been tackled. If a man and woman are not fulfilled when they enter a marriage they are unlikely to be fulfilled within the marriage.

Healing from childhood hurts, which frees us to move towards a fulfilling relationship, involves not only facing and coming to terms with those hurts but moving from a position of blame. Whilst we continue to hold onto bitterness towards parents, others or circumstances, this will taint relationships. There is a need not only to feel and face our hurts, but also to look at our reaction to those hurts and the way we carry defensive attitudes into adult life.

Negative attitudes

Pain easily grows into a negative attitude which can be destructive to us and to others. The erosion is so subtle that it can develop without a person realising. This diminishment might be as a result of our own thoughts or could be made worse by parental or peer pressure.

Other people's attitudes can affect us. 'She's such a nice person, isn't it a shame she hasn't found a man?' onlookers may say. And shame is exactly what we may feel; the feeling that we are 'bad'. Another comment made is: 'She's such a caring person, isn't it a waste that she isn't married?' The implication here is that the caring can only be directed towards a husband and children. Can it? Not marrying may also be seen as letting people down and denying our parents the pleasure of being grandparents.

A passionate longing for, and preoccupation with, marriage is picked up by others and affects the way they see and treat the person. Someone with a negative attitude, feeling he/she doesn't fit in, can evoke a feeling of pity in others which is patronising. Or it can cause others to draw back, finding it difficult to mix with someone who is negative and self-absorbed. The disappointment, misery and bitterness which some singles reveal can create a character which becomes less and less attractive. On the other hand, someone who is fulfilled and making the most of life has a chance of attracting people and increasing their circle of friends.

It is not 'wrong' to feel pain over not being married, but the damage comes when the person drops down into the pool of pity, where everything is judged according to the longing for a partner. If we are not careful the desire for marriage can become an obsession. It is like a starving person who thinks of little else other than food, and whose whole life revolves around these thoughts. The single person can start to think in terms of going to a certain function or church in case there is a potential mate there; looking at every unmarried person of the opposite sex in the light of their 'suitability'.

In our search for a partner and our pain over things 'not working out', we can put ourselves in a place of hating life, hating others and hating ourselves. Seeing younger siblings or friends the same age get married may cause one to lose heart and feel that life is unfair. Let-downs and break-ups in relationship can result in becoming embittered. Beliefs about how we *ought* to be able to find 'Mr/s Right' by a certain age may lead to cynicism. Jealousy and envy can so easily be stirred as one looks at the married couple, the newly-born baby, the child who throws his arms around his mother and says, 'I love you, Mummy'. Engagements, weddings, new homes – all can add to the blackness of the single state and the feeling that marriage is a futile dream which becomes a reality for everyone but *me*.

For some people, there is not only a negative attitude towards singleness, but towards themselves and their mistakes. When we disappoint others, or let ourselves down, we have a choice: either to keep 'lying on the floor', kicking ourselves, or picking ourselves up. The ground is not a comfortable place for too long, yet many stay there, feeling the grit grind into their skin. Even the prodigal son eventually had the courage to pick himself up and go back to his father. What he received, through that act of courage and willingness to expose himself and face his behaviour, was far greater than he could have imagined and certainly more than he would have received back in the pigsty.

Shortly before Christmas a woman in her forties rang me. 'I suppose I will be on my own again,' she said in a very sad voice. It wasn't the first such phone call from her that I had received. I could understand her pain but presented the many alternatives. For each one she found a reason as to why it wouldn't work. She was feeling sorry for herself and she wanted others to do likewise. She put herself in the position of being the victim who needed to be rescued from her dreadful plight. I wonder whether she would have enjoyed any of the alternatives, even if she had dared to take them? If ever we are consumed by a similar attitude, maybe we need to ask ourselves: 'Am I trying to punish myself or other people through guilt and manipulation?'

> A professor once said, 'A person wrapped up in himself makes a very small package.' This is true, but it is also true that a person wrapped up in himself is in a very strong prison. One becomes locked up in 'self' by concentrating on one's hurts and their consequences.
>
> The man or woman who dwells on all the negative things that have happened to him will soon become

> obsessed with 'me', 'myself' and 'I'. Everyone he meets will become an audience to his tale of woes. In what sense is this person in bondage? God has called us to love and serve others. A man imprisoned in himself is unable to give himself to others. He is not free to do what God has called him to do.[2]

A negative attitude towards singleness and towards oneself can also mean a negative attitude towards other people, specifically or in general. One can find fault with whatever alternative is offered, other than the 'ideal', or towards everyone we meet. We find excuses: 'This person isn't right because ...' or 'That won't work because ...' As Nicky Cruz once pointed out: 'A critical spirit may begin with one or two people, but left to grow within, it spreads like the mustard seed. Eventually we are critical of everyone we meet. Soon we shut out those around us, and we don't even know why. In return they shut us out, and there we are. All alone, and oh, so lonely.'[3]

Some single people who are looking for the 'right person' are never satisfied because they have not accepted that others are different. Without realising it, they are looking to the other person for their own way of approaching things. When a different approach is expressed the person is considered 'not right'. Yet, 'Love is not primarily a relationship to a specific person; it is an *attitude,* an *orientation of character* which determines the relatedness of a person to the world as a whole, not towards one "object" of love. If a person only loves one other person and is indifferent to the rest of his fellow men, his love is not love but a symbiotic attachment ...'[4] In life we may meet people who are 'not our type' and yet we can learn from them. We may not share the same lifestyle or outlook, and they may not be the person we would want to marry, but mixing with them can broaden our understanding. Life is an education and the more experiences one can have, some of which might be difficult, the better equipped we are.

Positive attitudes

A positive attitude towards singleness does not mean that longings don't exist. In reality, it probably means that life will consist of cycles of hope and despair, but the lower moments are used for growth.

A positive attitude towards singleness is to see its good points in perspective and to see the desire for marriage as a *part of life* rather than *life itself*. It is about viewing both marriage and singleness realistically, learning to get the most out of the moment and using our singleness to our advantage, instead of allowing it to be a weight which crushes us. Roy, a divorced man in his fifties, recounts what must be the most commonly recognised benefit of being single: 'Freedom and contentment in being able to do what I want.' I have to admit that 'freedom' is what keeps me going in the single life! Shirley, who has been on invalidity benefit for some time and struggles to make ends meet, said that one of the positive aspects of being on her own and free in the daytime is that she is able to visit the elderly and housebound.

A positive attitude is different for each individual person but one simple definition of it is gaining through losing and using pain to create enrichment. It is easy to think: 'If I *knew* I'd be getting married in two years I could throw myself into the single life now.' The same is true of so many other situations: if we knew the future maybe we would use the present more to our advantage. But we don't know and we can't know. The uncertainty and 'not knowing' so often keep a person living with the pain of what is missing rather than living in the pleasure of the moment. Despite our 'not knowing' we need to live in a state of *life* not *longing*.

When one has a strong desire for marriage it can be

very difficult to face and accept one's current state of singleness as best. The single person may need consciously to choose singleness at that time in their life in order to cope with emotional issues. Sara is in her mid-twenties and has chosen both to live with a family and to remain single, 'as opposed to lamenting over finding male-female relationships difficult or always to be looking for "would-be" partners'. Her choice came out of the recognition that she needed to come to terms with her father's suicide and her history of sexual and emotional abuse before she could ever consider the giving of herself in a marriage relationship.

In order to handle the frustrations of singleness we need to find out what kind of help works best for us so that we can learn to enjoy our current state. As Chris, a divorced woman in her mid-thirties said: 'I try to be kind to myself and to focus on the good, positive aspects of life. I make the best of things and I carry a hope that one day I will have another opportunity to enjoy marriage, but I don't let the desire dominate me.' A friend of mine anticipated feeling lonely on her twenty-fifth birthday. She loved children and decided to have a party. She invited only children and everyone had a 'whale of a time'. She was both giving and receiving and soon felt rewarded rather than miserable.

Whilst marriage might be fulfilling, it is not the *source* of fulfilment. My faith has been the stable force in my struggle to accept singleness. Amongst all the uncertainty and unfulfilled desires is the fact that God has a plan and purpose for my life. I may know what I want, but as someone once said: 'Without a belief that God is *for* me, and that he knows what is best at this particular moment, I would find it incredibly difficult to accept my singleness and would dive into the nearest relationship.'

Trust in the Lord with all your heart,
and do not lean on your own understanding.
In all your ways acknowledge him,
and he will make your paths straight.
(Proverbs 3:5–6 NASB)

If you can find happiness despite marital status you can be happy whether you are single or married. We need to begin to let go of other people's expectations for our lives, what we think other people's expectations are, and what we have drawn up as the 'norm' as a result of those expectations.

We should take note of the positive aspects of life. Have you ever written a list of the pros of your current state? The thought of doing anything quite so constructive can sometimes create deep feelings of anger. 'I know there are positive aspects,' we scream inside, 'but I don't care. All I want is to find Mr/s Right!' The feeling can be so intense that we push aside any ways of looking objectively at the situation and simply live in a constant state of 'attack'. The same is true when we work through past hurts.

In counselling one finds that many people would rather let the counsellor know of the horror of the past (over and over again) than learn new ways of coping with the pain and eventually see release. There is something within so many of us that cries out to reveal to another 'just how terrible things are'. Though it is difficult, it is good to look at the whole of one's life, or the whole of one's day, and measure the good with the bad. During one difficult time in my life I started to keep a diary of 'nice things and new awakenings'. After only a week or two I began to see that most days there *was* something good, even if it was as simple as noticing a duck on the water with his bottom in the air! As time went by, ensuring that I looked at the positive every day helped to get my life more into perspective.

Not only do we need to look at the positive aspects of life but we need to learn to do things for ourselves; to take pleasure in doing things for our own satisfaction. Our lives may not necessarily be the way we want them to be, especially in relation to marriage, so we may need to accept that which cannot be changed and develop that which can be moulded into something new. We may plan for marriage but can we alter our plans, even if only temporarily? It's like planning to go to the beach and then it rains. Are we to stay at home and be miserable because our initial plan is not possible at the moment, or do we change plans and, although different, enjoy the new arrangement?

We also need to listen to ourselves, to discover what our current priorities are. I may say I want to get married and proclaim that this is something for *now*, when, in reality, there are other priorities in my life and marriage is for later. What do I believe are the pros and cons regarding marriage for me now? Are there areas in my life which it would be beneficial to look at before considering marriage? Answering similar questions and taking small progressive steps, not massive leaps, in a particular direction will lead us positively forward. A wise man wrote: 'I am not what I should be, and I am not what I am going to be, but I am not what I was.' We are always changing.

A large part of the gradual move from the negative to the positive view is to look at, and alter, the way we see success and failure. So often our thinking is very black and white:

marriage = success
singleness = failure

university = success
no university = failure

good earnings = success
poor earnings = failure

homeowner = success
non-homeowner = failure

Looking at the above examples, I would presently be classed as a failure on all four accounts! But I don't consider myself a failure since, at the age when many writers are just starting their careers, (30) I have already had four books and numerous articles published and spent four years as an editor. Perhaps we need to change our value systems, or challenge the world's. Success has more to do with *what we make of our opportunities* and the character we develop than it has to do with our position in the world. This philosophy is an essential element to singleness being viewed as a 'good' experience.

Acceptance, and learning to live

We need to let go of being anxious about our single state, though we may still have longings. Peace comes in the *surrender* of our desires not the *denial* of our desires. As Julia Duin points out:

> In *Through the Looking Glass,* Lewis Carroll illustrated the principle of reaching our goals by surrendering our rights to them. He shows Alice heading towards a hill in the middle of a garden, but every time she heads straight for the hill, she ends up farther away. She is finally advised to walk away from the hill and to her surprise, she soon ends up at the base of it. The pain and dying to ourselves in small, everyday sacrifices clears our vision for what is truly precious in life.[5]

I mentioned in Chapter 3 Jephthah's daughter, who asked her father if she could go to the hills to weep about the fact that she would not marry. In reading the passage

(Judges 11) we also see that she submitted to what could not be changed. Submitting to what we cannot change (right now) is quite different from living in a constant state of fighting against it and being miserable. Accepting singleness instead of fighting it is very important. Surprisingly, it has often been the case that when true acceptance and peace have come, people suddenly find themselves with a marriage proposal on their hands. Let go and let God! Sometimes I wonder whether God wants to bring people to the point of being willing to walk the path of singleness for ever (a sacrificial surrender and honest desire to be obedient) before he will give them their heart's desire.

Carol, a South African friend, is a good example of this. Having been through a very painful time following a broken marriage, she remarried a divorced man who has the custody of his two children. Following my broken engagement she wrote to me:

> I was at my most cynical when I met Paul. I had lost all hope in the fact that God had something down the line for me. I had gone through a very angry time and had just had a spell in hospital. Spiritually I felt very alienated from the Lord. And yet it was then, in the midst of all that, that he stepped in. I really want to encourage you by saying that somewhere in all of this God sees the bigger picture for your life. You seem to have had one disappointment after another. I know what it's like to be where you're at, and it is so difficult to trust in those circumstances.
>
> My friend, I have found such happiness with Paul and the children. Paul is so stable and loving and caring. He treats me like a queen and is unbelievably good to me. My prayer for you is that the Lord will give to you what I have found. It's been worth all the pain, all the questions, and all the uncertainty.

Although my heart aches for what Carol has found, and I want to believe that God will fulfil my longings, I know that I must first be content with being single – content with being myself. In Cliff Richard's book *Single Minded* he points out three essential areas in his life which have enabled him to feel content with being single. I think they are important for all of us:

1. Fulfilment
2. Freedom
3. Friendship

Are we finding these in our lives? If not, can we help ourselves to find them? If we are not happy with the way things are, we need to be prepared to ask what we can do to change the situation. We need to spend time getting to know our strengths and weaknesses and to use these for our own, and other people's, good. We need to take a look at ourselves and ask some searching questions:

- How do I see fulfilment?
- Can I surrender my desires?
- Am I constantly on the 'look out' for the right person?
- Am I fighting my current situation?
- Are there past hurts I need to work through?
- Are there behaviour patterns, or ways of relating, I need to change?
- Am I frightened of freedom?
- Am I meeting a variety of people?

A lack of honesty and a failure to 'take a look' at ourselves often results in the suffering of singleness – a neurotic suffering. Neurotic suffering is more often than not due to incorrect thinking. We view life through the wounds we have encountered and it easily becomes distorted. Most distorted of all is our picture of ourselves. The result is that we walk into situations which only confirm our opinion and add to the pain. We become helpless victims trapped in unchangeable circumstances.

If we want a different experience of singleness we need a changed attitude. If the Church changes and the single person stays the same, nothing constructive can come about. Until we accept our present single state and discover that it is good, we will not find peace or happiness. We will continue to wrestle, and wrestling is pretty tiring when it occurs on a daily basis. It is easy to look at another person who seems to be gaining so much and enjoying his/her current state and feel 'I wish I could be like that'. But we can!

To change, we need to examine and understand our attitude and in what way it is interfering with enjoyment. We need to look at the way in which we interpret and value experiences, and the way in which we cover up our feelings. This requires openness – which can hurt. But hurts and sadness are all a part of *living*. Our lives should be moving, not static; we should be in a constant state of slight shift and growth. We also have to realise that there is a chance that what we desire we may, possibly, never have. 'Many things appeal and are desirable, but reality says you can't have them all'.[6]

Our ability to handle our single state has a lot to do with where our focus is. If our focus is on what we *haven't* got, then there will be much pain and frustration in our life; if it is on what we *have* got, then there is a greater chance of acceptance. True happiness is not a 'high' but a peace. Ezra Pound said: 'A slave is one who waits for someone else to come and free him.' Are we going to wait for the 'right person' to come and free us from the tyranny of singleness, or are we going to free ourselves by making the most of our lives?

Part 3
Finding freedom

8 | Constructive care

Singles need to be cared for in the Church in a way which helps them to make the most of their situation and enjoy life. The way in which a person is treated emotionally affects their reaction to life, to giving and receiving love, and to Christianity. Unfortunately, in some churches there is a need for drastic change concerning the treatment of *all* people, not just singles. In too many situations damage comes about when misguided Christians treat both other Christians and non-believers badly.

Many non-churchgoers say that it is not faith which presents a problem but the people: people who are judgemental, authoritarian, and concerned more about the details of one's belief than about the individual. A judgemental attitude crushes a person's spirit; and words of love without love in action leaves that person confused. Often the emphasis on one's spirituality becomes paramount; giving the impression that Christianity is more concerned with doing and saying the right thing than with who we are. It is so important to remind people that 'when they fall into sin, they also fall into the grace of God'.[1]

Affirmation

Constructive care means looking at the character of Jesus and working towards attaining his qualities for ourselves. It is to care about and be there for those we encounter, not only on a Sunday but during the week; it is to be a community of supportive people (even amongst those who are less well known to us). Recently a telephone caller, a stranger, asked to speak to a member of the family who own the house where I live. I said that no one was in. 'Are you lonely?' the caller asked. I was somewhat taken aback! As it happened I wasn't, so I replied 'No'. When the conversation ended I put the phone down and wished I had said, 'Thank you for asking'. I thought of the days when I *was* lonely; when being asked such a question, even by a stranger, would have made all the difference.

Constructive care is not merely about the Church providing the right facilities for the single person, although this is important, but about providing the right environment. To put it very simplistically, there are two types of church environment in which two different reactions are fostered. The first is a controlled environment, where errors are quickly picked up but effort is rarely praised. There is continual expectation for members to behave in a certain way (usually like the leaders), and the presentation is confrontational or legalistic. This often results, particularly for those who are sensitive, in a gradual loss of confidence, killing of spontaneity and lack of being oneself. The second example is a free environment where, although there are clear boundaries, members are encouraged to be themselves and are given responsibility for their own growth and errors. The individual's identity, as a person, is separated from his/her behaviour, and there is affirmation, which results in expression and acceptance.

To help people the Church needs to accept their current position and the experiences they are going through. The break-up of a relationship/marriage can be intensely painful and can leave a person facing loneliness, loss, chaos and crisis. Life can easily become fragile. The Church should help to encourage the person who is hurting to find acceptable ways of expressing his/her pain, rather than standing in judgement over the lack of faith or maturity and saying it is wrong to behave in a certain way.

Perhaps there needs to be more openness about our inner feelings, instead of the pretence of 'Now I'm saved my life is hunky-dory'. Occasionally it would be good to hear 'I am in the midst of a process and learning' testimonies, instead of 'I got saved and now life's wonderful'. Sometimes all that people who are struggling require is that other people recognise that the struggle is not easy. C. S. Lewis was a great man who stood in front of hundreds of people and spoke about pain, growth and trusting God. When deep suffering became a reality for him, through the death of his wife Joy, he was left for a period feeling disillusioned and questioning what he believed. It is so easy to hold to ideals of maturity and faith in the midst of suffering, until we ourselves are faced with that suffering. Our own suffering brings us face-to-face with our perception of other people and how they handle things.

Just as we need acceptance so we need to be heard. We also need to listen to others. Joyce Huggett believes that 'listening is a way of expressing our spirituality'.[2] There are two levels of listening: just hearing the facts, and hearing the feelings behind the facts. The latter level involves giving space, being non-judgemental, and understanding what the other person is trying to communicate. This is sometimes known as *active* listening: whilst it is not necessarily providing answers, it is far from passive. Active listening is healing for the one being listened to, and gives the listener a glimpse not only of what is being said but of the very essence of the person. A summary of the writings of The Samaritans in South Africa make the distinction crystal clear:

You are *not listening* to me when you …

- do not care about me
- say you understand before you know me well enough
- have an answer for my problem before I've finished telling you what my problem is

- cut me off before I've finished speaking
- finish my sentence for me
- find me boring and don't tell me
- feel critical of my vocabulary, grammar and accent
- are dying to tell me something
- tell me about your experience, making mine feel unimportant
- are communicating to someone else in the room
- refuse my thanks by telling me you haven't really done anything

You *are listening* to me when you ...

- come quietly into my private world and let me be me
- really try to understand me even if I'm not making much sense
- grasp my point even when it's against your own conviction
- realise that the hour I took from you has left you a bit tired and drained
- allow me the dignity of making my own decisions even though you think they might be wrong
- do not take my problem from me, but allow me to deal with it in my own way
- do not offer religious solace before I am ready for it
- give me enough room to discover for myself what is really going on
- accept my gift of gratitude by telling me how good it makes you feel to know that you have been helpful

As a Church we need to take an interest in each other as *people*. Gentleness, care, compassion, sensitivity and taking time to know a person before jumping in with advice are important. Proverbs says: *The right word at the right time is like precious gold set in silver* (25:11 CEV). To understand is to empathise, and to empathise is to step inside the hurting person's inner world, to get a feeling for what this world is like, and to look at the outer world through his/her eyes.

The ability to communicate the way we see the other person's world, but in a sensitive and tangible way, is also needed. We earn the right to confront another person by the amount of time and empathy we invest in that individual. Confrontation without really knowing the person, or without having invested sufficient empathy, results in that person experiencing any comment suggesting change as criticism. Constant criticism causes us to believe that we are bad. If others don't appreciate you it is difficult to appreciate yourself.

We all need affirming, consistent, unconditional love which helps us to rise above feelings of worthlessness, discouragement and pain. It is through a consistently accepting environment that change can take place. This type of love is known in the New Testament as *agape* love. 1 Corinthians 13:4–8 speaks of the nature of the love we should seek to demonstrate – an active and moving love:

> *Love is kind and patient, never jealous, boastful, proud or rude. Love isn't selfish or quick-tempered. It doesn't keep a record of wrongs that others do. Love rejoices in the truth, but not in evil. Love is always supportive, loyal, hopeful and trusting. Love never fails!* (CEV)

Love heals in a way which nothing else can. Betty, who is in her sixties, said that she has been helped a great deal by 'being loved when I felt unlovable, which gave me courage, peace and self-respect'. To love is to see the potential in another person. Love longs to see the person free from pain and sin, but does not stand in criticism because of that pain and sin. We need to *show* others that we love, not just say that we do. C. S. Lewis, in his book *The Four Loves,* said: 'We must try to relate the human activities called "loves" to that Love which is God a little more precisely than we have yet done.'[3] Scripture teaches us to:

- love one another (John 13:34)
- not judge one another (Romans 14:13)
- build up one another (Romans 14:19)
- accept one another (Romans 15:7)
- care for one another (1 Corinthians 12:25)
- bear one another's burdens (Galatians 6:2)
- be kind to one another (Ephesians 4:32)
- forgive one another (Ephesians 4:32)
- comfort one another (1 Thessalonians 4:18)
- encourage one another (1 Thessalonians 5:11)
- be hospitable to one another (1 Peter 4:9)

... let it be the hidden person of the heart, with the imperishable quality of a gentle and quiet spirit, which is precious in the sight of God. (1 Peter 3:4 NASB)

Help

A growing area, and one which is very much needed, is a confidential listening and counselling service. Some churches offer a listening service, whilst others have a counselling centre or a list of centres to which people can be referred. A church is a place where people should feel free to talk, but not be pressurised to do so. Above all, churches are places which should teach people to live in the Truth. Often when people become born-again they are not taught to live it out – daily to take on board who they are in Christ, and to keep their focus on Jesus.

The way in which the Church can aid the hurting single person specifically is by helping him/her discover the *source* of the pain or difficulty. It is easy to assume that one feels down because of being single, but there may be emotions which can be traced to other experiences. Singleness may *accentuate* the pain rather than be the cause of it. Wherever the pain stems from, the fact is that the single person who seeks help is in pain. Some years ago I interviewed Dr Frank Minirth, the co-founder of the Minirth-Meier clinic, a Christian psychiatric clinic in Dallas, Texas. He said, 'Many people have strong feelings that they have never dealt with, and bringing them to the surface is akin to opening up a bad wound.' In medical practice one 'would slice the wound with a knife'. 'The pain would be excruciating, but once the pus had drained out the person would begin to get well.'[4] It is similar in emotional surgery. The wound cannot fail to be infected and tender whilst the pus remains. Exposure is an uncomfortable but releasing experience.

The kind of care which many churches offer is prayer counselling, which can be very supportive to people. But in caring for people we need to be sensitive to their position. I often receive letters from people who are in great pain because they are too shy or fearful to ask verbally for help. Such people often indicate indirectly that they need support. We must be sensitive enough to come alongside them and ask if we can be there for them in any way. Sometimes it is merely companionship, encouragement, affirmation or even a cuddle that the person requires. We need to truly listen to one another and acknowledge any pain and heartache caused by loneliness, loss, change, searching, vulnerability, sexuality, an identity crisis, etc.

Constructive care is to care for the *whole* person – body, mind and spirit – and to help the individual to guard against anything which lowers their ability to cope, e.g. lack of sleep, poor diet, stress, lack of spiritual nourishment, lack of interaction with people, etc. In caring for the body the Church needs to help people to look after themselves adequately – the body being the Temple of the Holy Spirit. In caring for the mind the Church needs to teach about the renewal of the mind (Romans 12:2), standing against the lies of the enemy. People need to be helped to understand and deal with specific problems in their lives. In caring for the Spirit, the Church needs to teach people to take on board the truths of Scripture.

But however much support the Church offers the single person in times of need, it is still up to the single to be honest as to how he/she feels. The individual must define and express needs, and take personal responsibility. The church should not have to play the guessing game. One Church, in an attempt to understand the needs of its members, and to minister to those needs, gave out questionnaires for members to answer. The members were then visited, with time to talk about their answers. The church took the opportunity to find out what people's needs were, rather than assuming that they knew or deciding what was best.

Groups

One place we can find friends, learn to relate and feel accepted is in a group situation. In groups one can usually find some like-minded people, or at least people who are facing the same challenges in life. Groups are a point of contact and can be approached without an invitation. They often have specific meeting times and a structure, enabling a member to have a definite date for the diary and a reason to go out. How much a person gets out of any particular group depends on various things – how much he/she puts into the group, the personality of the individual and whether he/she is comfortable and is relating to the group, the person's spiritual and emotional state, the other people in the group.

Some churches provide singles' or young adults' groups. Do such groups help? Opinions vary, but so much depends on the group itself, the attitude and input of its members, and the way the group is handled by the leadership of the particular church. Whilst youth groups seem to work quite well, young adults' groups frequently fail. There is often a stigma attached to such a group and young people nearing the age of joining look upon it as the place for 'odd-bods' or 'fuddy-duddies'. Why? Perhaps it's because some members are a little old-fashioned in appearance and outlook, or because the group is so spiritual people find it difficult to relate to it, or because it lacks an interesting programme. In one such group the younger members objected to a few 'out of touch' older members. They proposed to the church leadership that all members over thirty should be 'chucked out'. I was twenty at the time and could see their point. But by thirty, one sees beyond the image to the individual and the personality.

A 'singles only' group creates a division by separating singles and marrieds. In a singles' group there can also be pressure to form long-term relationships with the opposite sex – so many single groups are regarded as matchmaking outlets. The New Testament stresses the unity of the Church (one body) and so maybe it is not helpful to have anything which runs against this concept. Some young adults' groups are open to both marrieds and singles and this tends to bring about a healthier balance. Sadly, most singles' groups are aimed at a particular age group; but what about the 'not so young' adults? How does the Church cater for them? Besides, when does one cease to be 'not-so-young'? Each person is different and the rate of maturity varies. It seems that whatever kind of group the Church tries to create for its members someone doesn't quite fit in. It is unlikely that there is an ideal solution.

One factor to bear in mind is that, whatever the definition of the group, it will not be static. A group will change according to its members: the types of people, their ages, interests and needs. Many church groups go wrong because they try to do things 'the way they have always been done', resulting in stagnation. Such groups need to be flexible and let the members dictate according to their current needs. Feedback should be positively encouraged. Unfortunately so many people lack a vision for their groups. Each member should ascertain what they want out of the group and what they are prepared to put into it. It isn't fair or constructive to moan about a group if we are not prepared to do something to bring about change. Change rarely 'just happens': it requires assessment and effort. The point of a group is the growth and stimulation of its members. To ensure a group doesn't become a 'pity-party', boring, a closed clique, or insensitive to newcomers or those who find it hard to relate or participate, members have to be willing and able to give of themselves.

Perhaps instead of a young adults' group the Church could create a variety of groups based on interests and hobbies, open to both marrieds and singles. It might also be helpful to have a place where people can drop in. Recently I attended an informal art group for people of all abilities. The tutor spoke briefly about art history and then people came and went, doing their own thing. As I sat there I thought about how nice it would be if something similar existed in a church context. Instead of the short talk about art history – or in addition to it – there could be one which related to our spiritual lives.

Apart from groups, how else can the Church provide constructive care for individuals? By:

- allowing people to express their thoughts and opinions
- creating an opportunity for greater openness about struggles
- creating an opportunity for discussion and teaching on sexuality
- visiting those who find it hard to get out due to illness, fear or old age
- offering practical, as well as spiritual, help
- encouraging a balanced life of work, rest, spiritual input, relating, and recreational activities

- encouraging the making of friends, and having open homes
- encouraging people to mix (married and single, young and old, male and female)

To encourage singles and marrieds to mix and benefit from one another does not mean the married couple using the single person as an easy-option babysitter, nor the single person using the married couple as a convenient meal provider (although these two acts of giving may be a part of an eventual friendship). Mixing with marrieds means discovering what each person can give to the other in terms of inner quality. A relatively new friend of mine says that she is deeply grateful for single friends who contribute to her children's lives: 'Bringing up a child is a huge responsibility, and especially a child who soaks everything up. I really value my single friends who spend time with my children, give to them emotionally and offer them stimulation.' One day she called round with her youngest child, who quickly fell asleep in her mother's arms. Knowing how, as a single person, one can have unfulfilled maternal feelings, she offered the sleeping child to me. It was a soothing, warming moment of love as I cuddled the little girl until she woke.

Teaching

Constructive care means presenting teaching in the Church in a way which catches the attention of people and helps them in everyday life. It also means assessing needs and teaching according to those needs. Many singles feel that there is a lack of relevant teaching on singleness and on how to live as singles. One church, whose membership is divided evenly between marrieds and singles, ran a workshop on the relationship between the two groups. The outcome was greater understanding of each other, and consequently, deeper friendships.

To encourage awareness of singleness the Evangelical Alliance introduced Singles Sunday. This is a day set aside for input on, and regard for, singleness. Just as on Mothering Sunday, when church services often revolve around the recognition of mothers, it is hoped that Singles Sunday will be a time when singles are noted. Whilst some people have spoken favourably of Singles Sunday, others have been more cautious – pointing out that such a day may encourage a victim mentality amongst single Christians (a point I touched on in Chapter 2). Whether Singles Sunday is eventually accepted or not, one aspect of singles teaching needed is that surrounding the area of sexuality.

Sexuality needs to be addressed for two reasons: to help the single person in any personal struggles, and to enable the single person to have a general understanding of sexuality and so be able to handle situations which arise. Having worked as a counsellor, I have listened to the most horrendous stories of sexual encounters. However, when I then return to the church it is as though I move into another world, where I am expected to be a single person who 'knows nothing'. For those of us who are involved in helping others or who have been through abusive situations, it can feel as though the church is an 'unreal' place which does not relate to the 'real' world. Often the 'real' issues remain unaddressed in the Church.

An abused person can feel, when told from the pulpit of the wrongness of sexual encounters, that he/she is a bad person. For some abused youngsters sex has become a way of life: a life where pain and pleasure are intertwined and inseparable, where guilt and self-loathing are the only means of coping. The lack of attention to these subjects, and sensitivity towards those who are affected, underlines a denial of exactly how tough it is in the world outside. Maybe we need to look at some of these issues and thus bridge the gap which exists between the softness encountered in the Church and the toughness in the world.

At least one church I heard about manages to combine a very positive attitude and teaching regarding singleness: 'In our church, the goal is not to build a strong single adult ministry: rather we are striving to build strong single adults who are ministers. Our final product is people not programmes.'[5]

Broad outlook

Constructive care is about encouraging singles to have a broad outlook and enjoy all aspects of living. It is about using one's time in a variety of ways (whilst still adhering to biblical principles), gaining experience of life and growing in faith. This may mean developing hobbies or using community services. A fulfilled life comes in all forms, and recreational activities are a part of that. Jo said that she had made many friends at a local dance group for singles. House parties, singles' weeks and holidays which encourage mixing through arranged activities have helped some people.

The measure of whether the care being offered is beneficial is shown by individuals growing emotionally, spiritually and socially. If this is the case, deep friendships reflecting unconditional love will be formed; there will be expression rather than repression, and people will be free to be themselves without fear of what others think.

For some people the Church has helped to fill a void created by being on one's own and has met more needs than simply their spiritual needs. Sally, who is divorced, said of her church: 'They never fall short with any kind of help.' We should be able to say that regarding all churches, and maybe one day we will. But the Church is made up of the people and so it is *we* who need to change.

9 | REALISTIC RELATING

Finding freedom from the bondage of 'waiting for it all to happen' means developing meaningful friendships. Genesis says: *Then the Lord God said, 'It is not good for the man to be alone ...'* (2:18 NASB). I am sure that the subsequent creation of woman was partly due to people's need for relating, not just man's need for a woman. The key word in this passage is *alone*. We all need to be loved, accepted and understood. There is a fulfilment found in genuine, caring friendship which is not found in any other way. We need friends of all ages and both sexes. Friendships with different ages help us to mature and have a fuller picture of life. Friendships with the same sex help us to feel understood. Friendships with the opposite sex affirm our sexuality. Friendships with children help us to see the world through a child's eyes, adding a richness and purity to life.

In our pursuit of friendship we need to make sure that any friendship develops out of a growing inner security. If we look to another person to make us feel better about ourselves we are in danger of losing the friendship. Friendship should not be a substitute for working through our problems, hurts or feelings of loneliness. True friendship frees us to share our joys and our sadness, our strengths and our weaknesses. It should enrich our life and personality, and broaden our horizons – and that of our friends. It should free us to be ourselves, not push us into a mould; enhance growth, not restrict it.

The basis of friendship

In life we have acquaintances and we have friends. The two can feel quite different. We can know many people and yet not have any close friends. Becoming acquainted is relatively easy, but forming genuine friendships is a different matter. Proverbs 18:24 says: *A man of many friends comes to ruin, but there is a friend who sticks closer than a brother* (NASB). We may know many people, but we all need a few people to whom we are special and who are special to us. It's also often true that we have friends who pretend to be such but are only so at their own convenience. There is a big difference between these 'friends' and devoted friends. Proverbs 17:17 says: *A friends loves at all times …* (NASB).

In life we have three types of friends:

- friends who give to us
- friends we give to
- friends where there is mutual giving and receiving

I have friends who are there for me in times of need, people who are pillars of strength. The relationship in this instance is mostly made up of them taking care of me. I also have friends for whom I do the same and I am mostly, or exclusively, there for them. Then I have friends with whom I can be mutually strong and weak. The relationship varies from day-to-day and need to need, but the friendship is fairly well-balanced. It is this type of friendship which is 'true friendship' and through which great reward comes. In true friendship both people are receiving nourishment. Friendship such as this, I believe, is the foundation of a successful marriage.

In this 'give and take' friendship, we need to be willing to give and to receive. To be a good friend we need to have known a good friend. We have to have loving acceptance demonstrated to us, in order to demonstrate it to others. As in a chain, where one link depends on the other, so in friendship: other people's love is a model for us, and we in turn demonstrate that love in other friendships. Friendships don't 'just happen'. I don't mean that they can't grow overnight, but something has to be put in for something to be taken out. The individual is responsible for his/her own happiness. We cannot rely on the other person to 'make' us happy. This means that to be a good friend, and to have a good friend, we need to be at peace and accepting of ourselves. 'The essential basis of friendship is not who we know, but who we are.'[1] If we struggle to accept and care for ourselves we may struggle within our friendships.

So what is it we really want in a friendship? What is it that brings us a deep satisfaction and fulfilment in knowing another person? I conducted a survey of the qualities and characteristics people appreciate or long for in a friendship. The top five qualities were:

- a sense of humour/fun
- trustworthiness
- loyalty
- honesty (with wisdom)
- understanding

One list which was sent in described very aptly the qualities of a good friend. It is someone:

- with whom you are always comfortable
- with whom silence is as special as talking
- who does *not* gossip about things told in confidence
- who sees beauty, love and patience in you
- who never tires of encouraging
- who is cheerful and ready for any good adventure
- who is willing to come and keep you company
- whom you can trust in all circumstances

- who is *not* tied to your apron strings and expects to know everything as a right
- to whom you will listen and from whom you will benefit if they tell you something you would rather not hear

Proverbs 19:22 says: *What matters most is loyalty …* (CEV). The New American Standard Bible uses the word 'kindness' instead of 'loyalty'. We realise the depth of friendship, and the importance of it, when we look at the meaning of the word 'kindness' in the Old Testament. According to Spiros Zodhiates the word 'kindness' in the Hebrew is *cheçed*. He describes it as 'one of the most important words in the Hebrew Old Testament …It is more the attitude of love which contains mercy'[2] David Johnson, author of *Reaching Out*, says: 'To the extent that our relationships reflect kindness, mercy, consideration, tenderness, love, concern, compassion, co-operation, responsiveness and caring, we are becoming more human.'[3]

Do we display these qualities ourselves? Perhaps if we bemoan the fact that we do not have close friendships we should not so much look at how others fail us but how we fail them. Jim Conway, author of *Friendship – skills for having a friend, being a friend*, says: 'Friendship is not an idea; it's an experience. So if the adventure is going to pay off, you need to make concrete changes in your actions toward other people.'[4] The way we are with people will affect the way they are with us. Friendships are not merely how often we socialise, but how much we give of ourselves and receive from our friends. True friendship involves appreciating the inner person, their qualities, rather than outer appearances – what a person does or how popular he/she is. There is something deeply warming about being appreciated by another and having someone take an interest in us. In friendships we need to hear that we are valued and we need to tell others that we value them. We feel closer to others, and they to us, when we stop trying to impress, and learn to be ourselves.

Proverbs warns us to guard against particular character traits in other people, but these are equally applicable to ourselves. We must guard against being:

- a gossip (20:19)
- hot-tempered (22:24–25)
- rebellious (24:21–22)
- greedy (28:7)
- immoral (29:3)

None of these can earn us respect in other people's eyes. It might be profitable when considering our character to ask ourselves some searching questions. Am I able to:

- feel with my friend in times of pain or difficulty?
- willingly help out in times of crisis?
- look beyond the behaviour to the hurt person?
- spend time listening without providing an answer or assessment?
- value and appreciate my friend's viewpoints when they are different from mine?
- be free from obligation or trying to be a certain way?
- express reality; be relaxed about 'being me' with my friend?
- share my strengths and weaknesses?
- share experiences about different areas of my life?
- keep confidences?
- express my love, care and concern?
- notice when my friend is in need or is hurting?
- be committed to my friend, whether he/she is pleasing me or not, is happy or sad?
- add to my friend's life and growth?

To maintain a friendship there needs to be sincerity, genuineness, acceptance, trust, sensitivity, consideration, forgiveness and flexibility on both sides. We need to spend time with, and listen to, each other; we need to be *real*, and to express ourselves. As a friend, the fruit of our caring should be to help the other individual to feel cared for, understood and enabled to move towards reaching his/her potential.

The quality of our friendships may be indicative of our own character's quality. We need to work towards possessing the fruits of the Holy Spirit:

- love
- joy
- peace
- patience
- kindness
- goodness
- faithfulness
- gentleness
- self-control

> ... those best equipped for friendship are those most prepared to stand alone. A person who is committed to stand firm for his convictions, whatever that costs in terms of popularity and social acceptance, is the person who can be counted on to stand firm in his personal commitments when that becomes costly. Personal integrity, the ability to say no graciously yet firmly, the capacity to stand alone under fire and not to cave in under peer-group pressure – those are attributes to be valued highly in our friends and carefully cultivated in our own lives.[5]

The backbone of friendship is commitment, and it is at this stage that a friendship is put to the test. Commitment means sticking by a friend in the hard as well as the more rewarding times. It requires consistency in contact and support. One of the problems with singleness is that it is easy to give up on a friendship when it becomes difficult. For those in a marriage, who believe that institution is for life, there can be a willingness to work through the difficulties. The result is often that, thanks to the hard work, the two people become closer. Within singleness there is frequently no commitment, and problems become a reason to end the friendship rather than tools to develop it.

In addition to working on our friendships we need positive input. A friendship should not have to be an endless path of 'working at it'. If commitment is the backbone of friendship, communication is the glue. Communication means not only keeping in touch but relating at a deep level. So many people have lost the art of deep conversation, of sharing at an intimate level. If we don't communicate and give our friendships time to explore how the individuals feel then our friendships are in danger of becoming shallow. There is a vast difference between being friendly and being a friend. There is a price to true friendship (giving of ourselves), and if the price isn't paid (superficiality), then the friendship could be classed as 'cheap'. Sadly, many people don't give of themselves and consequently never taste emotional intimacy.

We do not need to be friends with everyone. By that I mean that in life we will not be liked by all people and cannot spend our lives bending over backwards to be liked. For some people this is a real problem. The thought of a sharp word, a conflict, a misunderstanding sends them into a whirlwind of emotional pain. We *choose* our friends, and may need to be careful in doing so. A friend is not someone who criticises, pulls down, or uses and leaves you out at their own convenience. And yet it is surprising how many people stay in such situations and label it 'friendship'. Although we should forgive I believe we should expect to be treated as we ought to treat others and vice versa. The more we respect ourselves, the less we will allow ourselves to be trapped in destructive friendships.

Lack of self-respect means not only finding oneself trapped in destructive or unhealthy friendships, but walking into destructive or unhealthy friendships. It is generally believed that when starting relationships we subconsciously choose someone who is at the same level of emotional maturity, even if different in character. That is why it is not uncommon for two people with problems and past hurts to date each other. In the same way, we often choose partners who mirror our childhood experiences. Perhaps if we want someone more 'sorted out' we need to look first at how we can sort ourselves out.

There are two simple rules in developing friendships:

1. Don't put the other person down
2. Don't put yourself down.

For many of us the first is far easier than the second! But a good reason for not putting yourself down is that people find it harder to relate to someone who is constantly negative about him/herself. It becomes a drain on the friendship.

We all need to have people around us who believe in us, who affirm us in our times of doubt. But however good our friendships, there will be times when there is hurt or disappointment. There are perhaps two lessons to be learnt from this: first, friendships are fragile, and second, we need to know what it is to forgive and persevere. ... all human friendships are limited in their scope and reliability. Always our most important relationship must be with God.

... However, putting God first does not hurt human friendships. It can only strengthen them ... Those whose security is in God will not try to grab it from other people.[6]

Barriers to friendship

Many people long for the closeness and dependability of a friend but fail to find one because they put up barriers – sometimes without even realising. What are some of the barriers to good friendship?

Withdrawing or a lack of involvement due to fear of being hurt. Fear in this context usually arises out of bad past experiences, whether this is in friendship with either sex or in a committed relationship with the opposite sex. Our natural reaction when we have been hurt is to insulate our fragile centre. Some people choose to run from the pain, others choose to cover it up. Rather than present a weak, vulnerable self we protect ourselves and develop what are known as defence mechanisms. These may include withdrawal, manipulation, pushing down or denying feelings, projecting onto others how we really feel, feeling and behaving like a child, or showing to an extreme extent the opposite of how we feel.

Pearl, who is in her sixties, had been happily married for twenty-seven years. When the marriage ended in divorce her big fear was that she would never dare to give to another person in the same way as she had to her husband. Garth, who is in his thirties, had lacked confidence as a child. He had no siblings and had felt - and still does feel – a loner. He doesn't want to be this way but rejection by the only woman he has ever loved knocked his confidence and caused him to be fearful of involvement. Some people also pull back from friendship, or they keep friendship at a superficial level, due to a fear of *really* being known by another person.

To insulate ourselves from pain means putting up a façade, and thus the giving up of our true or private selves. The façade can lead to devaluation of the true self. Undoubtedly, our level of communication will be limited. How can communication be deep if people are merely relating to an 'outer layer' or 'public image'? One of my favourite book titles is *The Delicate Art of Dancing with Porcupines*.[7] It conjures up a wonderful picture of the difficulties of getting close to people who have their prickly defences hard in place. There must be a real art to ensuring that, without causing harm, *our* prickles slip between *their* prickles as we endeavour to approach them. Do we really want to spend time in such futile behaviour? Removing the prickles exposes a bare, tender skin. Is that something we are prepared to endure in order to have a deeper friendship?

Trying to be like another person. Trying to be like someone else means not being genuine in a friendship. Such a deceit will not work. Who are we trying to fool? Certainly the truth of the falsehood will be known deep inside us, and that will only compound our dishonesty with feelings of guilt and the fear of being 'found out'. We all need to be our unique selves and to allow people to know us. Seeking to impress others is a sure way to kill a friendship. It is usually a slow death too, as the façade slides off and reveals real motives. When we stop trying to be like or to impress other people and allow ourselves to be ourselves, there is great freedom. It is as though life takes on a new dimension.

Believing one shouldn't have close friendships with the opposite sex. A person may have a problem about friendship with the opposite sex if there has been a bad experience in the past, in childhood or adulthood. There may have been an experience of abuse, violence, domination, control, etc. Yet others simply 'believe' that there is something essentially wrong with close male-female friendships. Some people suggest that this type of friendship should only develop within the context of a group. If a man and a woman are seen to develop a friendship outside a group, people automatically assume that it is a more meaningful relationship. Yet it *is* possible for a man and a woman simply to be friends. Relating to both sexes with integrity and purity is most important. The more relaxed we are in our relating, the more likely we will be to make a friendship which moves towards marriage. However, marriage should not be our motivating factor for such a friendship.

Not accepting singleness. If a person has not accepted his/her current state of singleness it may be hard to make good, healthy friendships with both single and married folk. It can be difficult to be friends with single members of the opposite sex if a person is always looking at them as 'datable material'. Relaxed friendship with a married person may also be difficult if one is always envious of his/her situation.

Lack of emotional separation from parents. This is perhaps a less obvious barrier to friendships, but still relevant. The lack of separation is sometimes due to the adult child's insecurity or inability to let go. At other times either or both parents may not have allowed their child to grow up, be independent and separate. Control and manipulation can be used to 'keep' an adult child, and ultimately this interferes with the person's healthy independence. Some single people simply cannot develop a life of their own without their parents constantly influencing their decision-making or needing to know what they are doing. Adult children *need* to separate from their parents – emotionally, practically, financially, and in terms of decision-making. Emotional deprivation in childhood can also result in that person relating to friends in a parent-to-child, rather than an adult-to-adult manner. Ultimately, friendships will not be sustainable unless the adult child overcomes the strong parental bonds and stands apart as a separate person.

Lack of social skills. People sometimes don't have close friends because they have not learnt how to relate. They may not have been encouraged to relate as children and now find it hard to feel close and to express themselves. Parents who have not had many friends will not have laid a very good foundation for their children to learn about friendship. Children or teenagers who are unhappy or depressed may miss out on the vital process of learning about, and being confident with, interaction.

Shyness or lack of confidence – whether it is through poor skills, past hurt or low self-esteem – is a destroyer of friendship. Yet sustaining conversation for some people is painful. Katie, a young girl I counselled, said that after the initial 'hello' with people she didn't know what to say. Part of the problem of being unable to make conversation was that she felt 'blank' in her personality. Apart from small talk, we tend to speak through our personality so it was no wonder she found it such a strain. The best conversation comes as a result of being confident in ourselves and confident in life.

For those who are shy, non-assertive or have a lack of identity, being with people who can help them come out of their shell or attending a class which enhances these skills can be beneficial. It is never too late to undo the damage, relearn skills and start afresh.

Although these defences help us to avoid pain, in the long run such avoidance only adds to our problems. Pain exists initially as an indicator that something is not right. It is better to acknowledge the pain, uncover its source, deal with its consequences and live a relatively pain-free life.

Subtle differences

We are not just people – we are male and female, and this means we are different ... Instead of showing that our differences do not make us unequal, some people try to pretend there are no differences at all ... If two groups of people can be proved to be different from each other in some way that we think is important, we believe we can treat them differently ... if the difference does not mean we should discriminate, what does it mean instead? The answer is simple. It means we need one another.[8]

As we make friends with both sexes and as we develop meaningful relationships which might lead to marriage, it is helpful to look at the way the sexes differ. Lack of insight so often leads to misunderstanding. Gary Smalley sums up the key differences between men and women as:

- mental/emotional
- physical
- sexual
- intuitive

Smalley's books, *For Better or for Best* (for women) and *If Only He Knew* (for men), are intended for those who are married; however the material is equally valuable for the single person seeking to interact with the opposite sex or to develop a relationship. Here are his views on the four key differences between the sexes:

Mental/emotional differences. Women tend to be more 'personal' than men. Women have a deeper interest in people and feelings, while men tend to be more preoccupied with practicalities that can be understood through logical deduction.

Dr Cecil Osborne says that women tend to become 'an intimate part' of the people they know and the things that surround them; they enter into a kind of 'oneness' with their surroundings. A man relates to people and situations, but he usually doesn't allow his identity to become entwined with them. He somehow remains apart ... Because of a woman's emotional identification with people and places around her, she needs more time to adjust to change than a man does.

Physical differences. According to Dr Paul Popenoe, founder of the American Institute of Family Relations in Los Angeles, a book could be filled with the biological differences between the sexes, excluding those differences related to reproduction.

Men and women differ in every cell of their bodies. This difference in the chromosome combination is the basic cause of development into male or female as the case may be.

Women have greater constitutional vitality, perhaps because of this chromosome difference ... Women's basal metabolism is normally lower than men's ... The thyroid gland behaves differently in the two sexes. Women's thyroid is larger and more active ... Women's blood contains more water than men's (20 per cent fewer red cells). Since the red cells supply oxygen to body cells, women tire more easily and are more prone to faint ...

Sexual differences. Women's sexual drive tends to be related to their menstrual cycle, while men's drive is fairly constant ... Women are stimulated more by touch and romantic words. They are far more attracted by a man's personality, while men are stimulated by sight ... While a man needs little or no preparation for the bedroom, a woman needs to be emotionally and mentally prepared ... Her preparation requires tender consideration, while harshness or abusive treatment can easily remove her desire for days at a time ...

Intuitive differences. What exactly is this 'woman's intuition'? It's not something mystical; rather, it is an unconscious perception of minute details that are

> sometimes tangible, sometimes abstract in nature. Since it is usually an 'unconscious' process, many times a woman isn't able to give specific explanations for the way she feels. She simply perceives or 'feels' something about a situation or person, while a man tends to follow logical analysis of circumstances or people.[9]

Women are also said to be more prone to depression than men. Dr James Dobson in *Man to Man about Women* says:

> Depression is not uniquely characteristic of women, certainly. But it occurs less frequently in men and is apparently more crisis-oriented. In other words, men get depressed over specific problems such as a business setback or an illness. However, they are less likely to experience the vague, generalised, almost indefinable feeling of discouragement which many women encounter on a regular basis.[10]

Maybe men need to understand this in order to stand by and have patience with women. A survey which Dr Dobson carried out amongst women revealed that low self-esteem was indicated as their most troubling problem. Perhaps women's propensity to depression has something to do with the way they communicate their feelings. There certainly seems to be quite a difference between the sexes when it comes to communication.

> Men are more proud than women and have greater difficulty in admitting their being afraid ... women often display their fears quite openly while men hide theirs ... speech itself has a different meaning for men than it has for women. Through speech men express ideas and communicate information. Women speak in order to express feelings, emotions ... Once a psychologist, in comparing married life to theatre, made the

> following remark, 'Love, for the woman, is itself the drama; for the man, it is the intermission.'[11]

There are countless areas where the sexes differ. Intelligence and mental capacity are often used to point out differences.

> Psychologists have known for decades that there is no fundamental difference in the overall level of intelligence between men and women, although there are areas of greater strength for each sex. Men tend to score higher on tests of mathematics and abstract reasoning, while women excel in language and all verbal skills ... women are much more inclined to doubt their own mental capacity than men.[12]

Male and female complement one another and so in the company of the opposite sex we more fully experience ourselves and our sexuality. Erich Fromm points out:

> There is masculinity and femininity in *character* as well as in *sexual function*. The masculine character can be defined as having the qualities of penetration, guidance, activity, discipline and adventurousness; the feminine character by the qualities of productive receptiveness, protection, realism, endurance, motherliness. (It must always be kept in mind that in each individual both characteristics are blended, but with the preponderance of those appertaining to 'his' or 'her' sex.)[13]

Do we take time to know and understand the opposite sex? Understanding each other will improve our relationships, whether they lead to friendship or marriage. And when our relationships are fulfilling they bring meaning to, and improve the quality of, our lives.

Personality

No matter how much we try to understand them, we may *still* find it difficult to establish friendships with certain people. Why do some people get on our nerves more than others? Much of it is due to personality type, temperament or social style. We seek out people who are like us because we feel comfortable with them and possibly think in the same way. But we also need people who are different from us to give us a broader perspective on life and to expand our understanding of others and ourselves.

There are many different classifications of personality types. Hippocrates, the Greek physician and philosopher, suggested 2,400 years ago that people fit into four basic categories. People tend to be predominantly one type but have traits of another or others:

Sanguine: warm, buoyant, lively and 'enjoying' temperament
Choleric: hot, quick, active, practical and strong-willed temperament
Melancholy: analytical, self-sacrificing, gifted, perfectionist temperament with a very sensitive emotional nature
Phlegmatic: calm, cool, slow, easy-going, well-balanced temperament[14]

A modern version of personality typing is the Myers Briggs Type Indicator (MBTI)[15] which lists sixteen different types. According to the MBTI, we are made up of a combination of four of the following:

E: Extraversion	or	I: Introversion
S: Sensing		N: Intuition
T: Thinking		F: Feeling
J: Judging		P: Perceiving

Although a person may have traces of the opposite within him/her, one will be dominant, e.g. one is classed as *either* an extrovert or an introvert, *either* sensing or intuitive. One's classification will not have extraversion *and* introversion, etc. Some of the indicators are:

E: Breadth of interest	I: Depth of concentration
S: Reliance on facts	N: Grasp of possibilities
T: Logic and analysis	F: Warmth and sympathy
J: Organisation	P: Adaptability

I have attended several courses where the MBTI or other personality type indicators have been used and have found it very helpful in understanding how and why I operate differently from another type of person. As we discover more about our personality type we discover more about our strengths and weaknesses. We can learn about roles best suited to us and about working as a team, complementing one another. Insight into personality type can help us to be more in touch with needs, more understanding of reactions and more conscious of developing opportunities. The dangers are that we don't take into consideration the uniqueness of the individual or that we use our personality type as an excuse.

Realistic relating is learning to accept people as they are; learning to appreciate others, even if they are quite different. It is about finding ways of being and feeling safe – physically and emotionally. Safe enough to be ourselves; safe enough to be a good friend without having to retreat, protect, cover up or impress.

The aim of this chapter has been to expose the areas in our lives which may prevent us from forming a deep relationship, which in turn brings satisfaction. The goal is to help us look at ourselves in a way which promotes change. We can never stop growing and maturing when it comes to character. The end result of these changes may be marriage or it may be singleness, but in either case the hope is that it will be contentment.

10 | Positive Pain

To laugh is to risk appearing the fool.
To weep is to risk appearing sentimental.
To reach out for another is to risk involvement.
To expose feelings is to risk exposing your true self.
To place your ideas, your dreams, before a crowd is to risk their loss.
To love is to risk not being loved in return.
To live is to risk dying.
To hope is to risk despair.
But risks must be taken, for the greater hazard is to risk nothing.
The person who risks nothing does nothing, has nothing and is nothing.
They may avoid suffering and sorrow, but they cannot learn, change, grow, love, live.
Chained by their attitude they are a slave, they have forfeited freedom.
Only a person who risks is free.

Anonymous

The journey

The single person is on a journey of risks. Any journey involves looking at where you are and where you want to go. The ultimate goal of the single's journey is fulfilment in all its aspects: fulfilment which brings about a new depth to life. As one looks at the route one discovers a maze of intertwined paths. On one path is marriage, on another children, on another work, on another friendships, on another ministry. Some people get to walk them all, whilst others walk only a few. It is impossible to compare the paths chosen, for the journey will never be the same for any two people. The journey varies from day to day and can be both wearisome and rewarding. Perhaps the most rewarding aspect is the realisation that even in the darkest moments we are not alone, though at times we walk the path with not a soul in sight.

There is one certainty about the journey, however – there will be pain. But pain is a motivating factor. It can drive us to look at our behaviour, to reassess our outlook on life, to draw closer to God. Whether or not pain drives us to do these things is our choice. We are the dictators of the direction. The same pain which produces richness in character in some can destroy other people. Pain is like putty: you can mould it into many things and use it creatively. If you don't mould it, it becomes hard and crusted and feels inflexible. Part of the journey is about making pain work for us, not against us. In order to make it work for us we have to let the pain out and use the energy in a creative way, rather than using the energy to keep a host of negative feelings from rearing their ugly heads.

We often demand that we are relieved from pain. Yet in our demand for relief we are also asking that our understanding of other people's struggles, and our refiner of character, be taken from us. Perhaps we should decide what we are trying to achieve in life. Happiness? Order? Pattern? All we long for? Marriage? Or are we working towards inner qualities? If we are working towards inner qualities we have to remember that suffering creates character. Certainly suffering for the sake of our faith does:

> *... Let us exult and triumph in our troubles and rejoice in our sufferings, knowing that pressure and affliction and hardship produce patient and unswerving endurance. And endurance (fortitude) develops maturity of character – that*

is, approved faith and tried integrity. And character (of this sort) produces (the habit of) joyful and confident hope of eternal salvation. Such hope never disappoints or deludes or shames us, for God's love has been poured out in our hearts through the Holy Spirit who has been given to us. (Romans 5:3–5 Amplified Bible)

On the journey there seem to be so many lessons to learn:

- Fulfilment is much more than having our needs met.
- One can lead a fulfilling life as a single person and still desire marriage.
- There needs to be intimacy in our relationships with others and in our relationship with God.

The reflective pools into which we gaze along our journey help us to discover more about life and its lessons. Some are pools of pain and suffering; others are pools of joy and release; however most are pools of learning and discerning. One of my moments of reflection has been discovering God's purpose for me. For the single Christian who desires to be married one of the most commonly quoted verses concerning God's promises is … *he will give you the desires of your heart* (Psalm 37:4 NIV). Yet without the first part of the sentence, '*Delight yourself in the Lord*', it becomes meaningless. The same principle of seeking God prior to receiving our desire applies too: *But seek first his kingdom and his righteousness, and all these things will be given to you as well.* (Matthew 6:33 NIV)

When my engagement was on the rocks, Psalm 37:4 spoke to me. I knew that, though I could see the engagement would fold and I desired marriage, I had to seek first the kingdom of God. I had to allow Him to be central in my life every day and walk in the Truth, before seeing fruit in my work and knowing the other things which would be added to my life. It brought a release in me and a confidence that what was right would come about. However, in the months leading up to this crisis I felt my confidence, in achieving what I was called to do through work, slipping, and my confidence as a person was crumbling through the disintegration of the relationship. At this point another verse was given to me: *So do not throw away your confidence; it will be richly rewarded. You need to persevere so that when you have done the will of God, you will receive what he has promised* (Hebrews 10:35–36 NIV). As I read those words the hope that my confidence in both work and personal relationships would be built up again was restored.

For me, as a Christian, fulfilment of desires does not occur in isolation from seeking God's will. Within the process of that seeking, a transformation takes place.

Transformation

I believe that the transformation comes about through faith and through experience in life, which enriches us. We cannot earn, buy or receive the transformation: we discover it. Carl Jung, the Swiss psychoanalyst and son of a clergyman, believed that 'Human thought cannot conceive any system or final truth that could give the patient what he needs in order to live: this is, faith, hope, love and insight.'[1] Our greatest experiences of healing are our ever-deepening faith; our ability to hold onto hope in the darkest moments; our living out unconditional love; and our insight regarding ourselves, others, life and God.

In Chapter 1, I talked about Dr Dan Montgomery's explanation of the four qualities of the healthy personality – love, assertion, weakness and strength – and how when we don't receive, or life upsets the balance of these qualities, we become anxious, manipulative, avoidant and artificial. I believe that when a life is transformed, instead of being artificial we become *real*. How? It seems to happen through wrestling with life's hurts and allowing our vulnerable self not only to be seen but, more important, accepted by others. We take off our masks and, instead of living as the 'strong coper' (despite feeling differently on the inside), we become the 'vulnerable, calm person'. The two aspects of ourselves (the one which longs and the one which can be objective) somehow become merged to create the real person. Joanne Smith, author of *How to Say Goodbye*, spoke of what becoming real meant to her following the premature death of her husband:

> As I became real, the character of my life changed. Areas of my identity I formerly thought needed to be sacredly preserved didn't. A part of who I am deep inside began to emerge with a new softness and depth of the character of Christ. I stopped picking up a script to act the part of the 'woman of faith' according to Joanne. My new-found vulnerability released me towards healing.[2]

The process of becoming real is very beautifully described in the story of *The Velveteen Rabbit* by Margery Williams:

> 'What is REAL?' asked the Rabbit one day, when they were lying side by side near the nursery fender, before Nana came to tidy the room. 'Does it mean having things that buzz inside you and a stick-out handle?'
> 'Real isn't how you are made,' said the Skin Horse. 'It's a thing that happens to you. When a child loves you for a long, long time, not just to play with, but REALLY loves you, then you become Real.'
>
> 'Does it hurt?' asked the Rabbit.
>
> 'Sometimes,' said the Skin Horse, for he was always truthful. 'When you are Real you don't mind being hurt.'
>
> 'Does it happen all at once, like being wound up?' he asked, 'or bit by bit?'

> 'It doesn't happen all at once,' said the Skin Horse. 'You become. It takes a long time. That's why it doesn't often happen to people who break easily, or have sharp edges, or who have to be carefully kept. Generally, by the time you are Real, most of your hair has been loved off, and your eyes drop out and you get loose in the joints and very shabby. But these things don't matter at all, because once you are Real you can't be ugly, except to people who don't understand.'[3]

What does becoming real mean?

- release
- expression
- aliveness
- love

Release. Release of feelings, frustrations, fears and needs; the ability to share openly and honestly what is going on inside us emotionally and bring things to God. Through the release we feel cleansed.

Expression. Expression of care and compassion towards others and ourselves; genuine expression of affirmation which restores others. Through the expression we feel gentleness.

Aliveness. Aliveness in all areas of human functioning – physically, emotionally and spiritually; aliveness which enriches our relating to others and to God. Through the aliveness we feel revitalised.

Love. Love in action which is without prejudice or expectation for love to be returned; love which leaves others wanting to love. Through the love we feel freedom.

Being real is not a one-off experience. It is being real every day, becoming more real every day. Being real brings about release, expression, aliveness and love in others as well; it enables them to be real too.

In order to become real we may have to change the way we see reality, which is difficult and costly. Dr John White, a psychiatrist and author, points out that facing reality is hard because the flesh fights against it. The insatiable and very deep need for love, inherent to mankind, and the consequent fear of rejection lie at the root of our fear of facing reality and our struggle to change. There are things about ourselves and others that we dare not face because we are afraid that reality may expose a lack of love for which we long.[4]

Transformation also involves a shift in our concept of love. Erich Fromm, possibly the greatest of the post-Freudian psychologists, believes that love is the only sane and satisfactory answer to the problem of human existence. He delves into the subject when he asks this very poignant question:

> Is love an art? Then it requires knowledge and effort … In the most general way, the active character of love can be described by stating that love is primarily *giving,* not receiving … Giving is the highest expression of potency. In the very act of giving, I experience my strength, my wealth, my power. This experience of heightened vitality and potency fills me with joy. I experience myself as overflowing, spending, alive, and hence as joyful. Giving is more joyous than receiving, not because it is a deprivation, but because in the act of giving lies the expression of my aliveness.
>
> The most important sphere of giving, however, is not that of material things, but lies in the specifically human realm. What does one person give to another? He gives of himself, of the most precious he has, he gives of his life. This does not necessarily mean that he

> sacrifices his life for the other – but that he gives him of that which is alive in him; he gives him of his joy, of his interest, of his understanding, of his knowledge, of his humour, of his sadness – of all expressions and manifestations of that which is alive in him. In thus giving of his life, he enriches the other person; he enhances the other's sense of aliveness by enhancing his own sense of aliveness. He does not give in order to receive ... But in giving he cannot help bringing something to life in the other person, and this which is brought to life reflects back to him; in truly giving, he cannot help receiving that which is given back to him. Giving implies to make the other person a giver also and they both share in the joy of what they have brought to life.[5]

Within transformation one reaches the point of having a thankful heart for *life* because life becomes so much broader than marriage. As one young man said: 'The key to the good life is selfless sacrifice to God and to others. Instead of expecting from others, one should seek out opportunities to do good to others.'

Discovery

As singles, to move from our searching for love in the 'right' person to the kind of loving which Erich Fromm talks of is to move from the prison of our aloneness. It is the beginning of our discovery. One's whole personality is transformed. What happens part-way along the journey is that you look at yourself and discover that a process has taken place and you have changed. You feel free.

What is the discovery? What is it we are trying to achieve? The place I am stretching out my hand to reach is the point of being *fully alive*. So many of us are half-dead: some are dead spiritually, others emotionally or relationally. Some are dead in their understanding, sensitivity, purpose, direction, communication. There is so much to life, so much to each individual, and so much yet to be brought alive. I felt greatly encouraged, having come to the realisation that the discovery is about being *fully alive*, when I read one of John Powell's books which talks about 'fully-alive human beings':

> Fully-alive human beings are alive in their external and internal *senses*. They see a beautiful world. They hear its music and poetry. They smell the fragrance of each new day and taste the deliciousness of every moment. Of course their senses are also insulted by ugliness and offended by odours. To be fully alive means to be open to the whole human experience. It is a struggle to climb a mountain, but the view from the top is magnificent. Fully-alive individuals have activated imaginations and cultivated senses of humour. They are alive, too, in their *emotions*. They are able to experience the full gamut and galaxy of human feelings – wonder, awe, tenderness, compassion, both agony and ecstasy.
>
> Fully-alive people are also alive in their *minds*. They are very much aware of the wisdom in the statement of Socrates that 'the unreflected life isn't worth living'. Fully-alive people are always thoughtful and reflective. They are capable of asking the right questions of life and flexible enough to let life question them. They will not live an unreflected life in an unexamined world. Most of all, perhaps, these people are alive in *will* and *heart*. They love much. They truly love and sincerely respect themselves. All love begins here and builds on this. Fully alive people are glad to be alive and to be who they are. In a delicate and sensitive way they also love others. Their general disposition towards all is one of concern and love ...
>
> Each tomorrow is a new opportunity which is

> eagerly anticipated. There is a reason to live and a reason to die. And when such people come to die their hearts will be filled with gratitude for all that has been, for 'the way we were', for a beautiful and full experience. A smile will spread throughout their whole being as their lives pass in review. And the world will always be a better place, a happier place, and a more human place because they lived and laughed and loved here.
>
> Fully-alive people, precisely because they are fully alive, obviously experience failure as well as success. They are open to both pain and pleasure. They have many questions and some answers. They cry and they laugh. They dream and they hope. The only things that remain alien to their experience of life are passivity and apathy. They say a strong 'yes' to life and a resounding 'amen' to love. They feel the strong stings of growing – of going from the old into the new – but their sleeves are always rolled up, their minds are whirring, and their hearts are ablaze. They are always moving, growing, beings-in-process …
>
> No person, including themselves, is today who he or she was yesterday. Since their vision is always tentative and open to modification, fully-alive people eagerly await new insights. These insights will renew them and their vision of reality.[6]

How does one reach this blissful state? John Powell points out five essential steps[7] into the fullness of life:

1. To accept oneself
2. To be oneself
3. To forget oneself in loving
4. To believe
5. To belong

I could write a whole book on these five elements alone! But for now let's take a briefer glimpse at how these might work out in practice.

To accept oneself. Many Christians think of accepting oneself as opposite to denying oneself, and since the Bible tells us to deny ourselves and take up our cross daily, accepting ourselves must be 'dangerous stuff'. I don't think so. Accepting oneself is a compliment to the Creator. Accepting ourselves is about being able to see our talents and good qualities and being grateful for these; being realistic about our failures and tendency to fall and looking at how we can change. It involves looking beyond the moments of bad behaviour to the pain underneath, and then dealing with the pain and wrong-doing tenderly through the love and forgiveness of God. A song by some friends, Charles and Nikki, described beautifully this concept. I find the first two verses alone bring freedom and acceptance for me:

Don't look at the woman
who's angry again;
look through to the child
who is crying with pain;
for abuse has a way
of abusing again.
Just tell me where
is the love
to cover all the shame?

Don't look at the man
who's been drinking again;
look through to the boy
who was abandoned at ten;
for rejection has a way
of rejecting again.
Just tell me where

is the love
to cover all the shame.

As we allow ourselves to see beyond our behaviour to the pain underneath, we are more able to do so with other people. To accept oneself is to treat oneself in the same way as we treat others. So often we have one set of rules for others and another for ourselves. Why is self-acceptance so important? Because it frees us not to need to seek out the attention of other people.

To be oneself. I am in the midst of changing to being myself and each day brings greater understanding. The discovery is exciting! The freedom to express *myself*, instead of feeling obliged to be the way others want me to be, is wonderful. A friend of mine, who did not know me before the change began to take place, commented on some old photographs: 'You look completely different.' I tried to explain it away by saying I had a different hair style or had lost weight, etc. 'No!' she replied, 'I can't quite put my finger on it. You've changed. I can see personality in you now.'

Being oneself is about having acquired sufficient self-acceptance for it to be alright to express oneself freely. It is being free to express emotions, thoughts, ideas; being free to make choices; being free to allow personality to show in the things we do, the clothes we wear and the choices we make. It is being real in a totally honest way. Being oneself is not for the sake of selfishness. God must be central in our actions for the good of others.

To forget oneself in loving. Perhaps another expression for this would be 'selfless loving'. I have a friend who has loved me through a series of crises in my life, through my getting better and beyond. In moments of darkness she held my hand, and in doubt she lifted me up. Cards of encouragement regularly came my way.

Instead of judgement over my behaviour came words of belief in me and my potential, and empathy for me in my struggles and pain. Love helps us to see the light, and to live again. Selfless, non-judgemental love is very healing. This kind of love is not about 'doing good', it is about giving of oneself.

We should each be seeking to be an example of love – a kind of love which has nothing to do with possessiveness, selfishness or manipulation. 'To love means to open ourselves to suffering. Shall we shut our doors to love, then, and be "safe"?'[8]

To believe. This, to me, is to have faith. It is about a meaning, a purpose, a direction. To believe in God and in his Son Jesus, and the divinity of Jesus, is to believe in eternal life for all who follow. To believe this is to know a depth in life that can be found in *nothing else*. It makes sense of our being on earth and of struggles in life. Hebrews 11:1 talks of faith as '*the conviction of things not seen*' (NASB). I don't think I could live without such a conviction. There is strength both *in* and *through* the believing. The power of the Holy Spirit enables us to live out our beliefs.

We need to experience the grace of God. But what exactly is grace? We talk about it glibly and maybe fail to realise its tremendous releasing power. In Christian belief, grace is the 'unmerited favour of God; a divine saving and strengthening influence'. Other words used to describe the Christian belief of grace are: goodwill, goodness, indulgence, forgiveness, favour, mercy, mercifulness, leniency, compassion, clemency, charity.[9] *Matthew Henry's Commentary*, explaining Jesus' words: *My grace is sufficient for you* … (2 Corinthians 12:9 NASB) says: 'Grace signifies two things: 1. The good will of God towards us, and this is sufficient to strengthen and comfort us. 2. The good work of God in us …'[10]

When we allow ourselves to stand in the grace of God it is evident to other people. Grace moves us towards wholeness. It can:

- bring us to a place of rest within ourselves
- help us when we have fallen
- give us a proper estimate of ourselves
- sustain us when we face trials in life
- give us a healthy perspective on life[11]

We have the choice to stand in the grace of God or to walk away in our own determination. But, as Elizabeth Elliot says: 'One who forfeits the grace of God is like a bitter, noxious weed which poisons the lives of others. Refusal to accept grace isolates, as a sulking child, wrapped up in his own misery, refuses comfort.'[12]

To belong. This is a longing which so many people have and some people fail to find. To belong is to be with like-minded people; to share at a deep level. It is to know committed friendship; to be a committed friend. Belonging comes in knowing the contentment of being 'at home' with another or a group of people. It is about sharing all that is most precious. We may still have the odd day when we are lonely, hurting, tempted – and we may have discovered ways of lessening the pain – but ultimately there is calm and peace within. The outcome is that we radiate calm and peace to others.

Although circumstances may not be perfect, and we may not have a partner, we can all know what it means to belong. For those who have chosen to be born-again as Christians, our sense of belonging is in the knowledge of who we are in Christ. This includes, amongst other things, being:

- a son (child) of God (Galatians 4:7)
- an heir to the Kingdom (Galatians 4:7)

- set free by Christ (Galatians 5:1)
- a new creature in Christ (2 Corinthians 5:17)
- redeemed (Galatians 3:13)

Freedom comes in keeping our focus on Jesus. The question we, as singles, must ask ourselves is not 'When is the right person going to turn up?' but 'Am I allowing my faith to be all it can be for me?' One word to sum up what we aim to achieve is *growth*. Growth comes about in a surprising way:

> I asked for strength – and God gave me difficulties
> to make me strong.
> I asked for wisdom – and God gave me problems
> to learn to solve.
> I asked for prosperity – and God gave me brain
> and brawn to work.
> I asked for courage – and God gave me dangers to
> overcome.
> I asked for love – and God gave me troubled
> people to help.
> I asked for favours – and God gave me
> opportunities.
> I received nothing I wanted; I received everything I
> needed.
> My prayer has been answered.
>
> Anon

Perhaps this is the ultimate lesson we need to learn as singles: we may or may not receive what we want, but we will receive what we need. It's a hard lesson but one with rich rewards.

REFERENCES

Chapter 1

1. L. Carter, P Meier and F. Minirth, *Why be Lonely?* (Grand Rapids: Baker Book House, 1982), pp. 49–51.
2. Figures from the Marriage Research Centre at the Central Middlesex Hospital, recorded in L. Harding, *Better Than or Equal To?* (Milton Keynes: Pioneer/ Word Books, 1993).
3. L. Frankel, *Women, Anger and Depression* (Deerfield Beach: Health Communications, Inc, 1992), pp. 15–16.
4. I. Tanner, *Loneliness: The Fear of Love* (New York: Harper and Row, 1973), p. 3.
5. F. D. Hammond, *Overcoming Rejection* (Chichester: Sovereign World, 1991), pp. 1–2, 4, 41.
6. Ibid., p. 93.
7. S. Page, *If I'm So Wonderful Why Am I Still Single?* (London: HarperCollins, 1993), p. 167.
8. Dr D. Montgomery, 'Love Beyond Betrayal', *Carer and Counsellor*, vol 3, no 2 (1993), p. 8. Adapted from Dr D. Montgomery, *How to Survive Practically Anything* (Ann Arbor: Servant Publications, 1993).
9. Ibid., pp. 9–10.
10. J. Smith and J. Biggs, *How to Say Goodbye* (Lynnwood: Aglow Publications, 1990), pp. 75–76.
11. L. Frankel, op. cit., p. 7.

Chapter 2

1. K. Keay, *Letters From A Solo Survivor* (London: Hodder & Stoughton, 1991), p. 140.

2. J. Duin, *Sex and the Single Christian* (London: Marshall Pickering, 1990), p. 17.
3. Ibid., p. 43.
4. L. Harding, *Better Than or Equal To?* (Milton Keynes: Pioneer/Word Books, 1993), p. 69.
5. N. Wright and M. Inmon, *Preparing Youth For Dating, Courtship and Marriage* (Eugene: Harvest House Publishers, 1978), p. 47.
6. J. Duin, op cit., pp. 114, 26.
7. J. Duin, op cit., p. 44.
8. F. D. Hammond, *Overcoming Rejection* (Chichester: Sovereign World, 1991), pp. 57–58.
9. L. Harding, op. cit., pp. 69–70.
10. M. Clarkson, *Single* (Eastbourne: Kingsway 1980), p. 123.
11. 'Angelo Grazioli talks to Helena Wilkinson', *Carer and Counsellor*, vol 4, no 1 (1994), pp. 39–41.
12. M. Quoist, *Prayers of Life* (Dublin: Logos Books, 1966), pp. 38–39.
13. J. E. Adams, *A Theology of Christian Counselling* (Grand Rapids: Zondervan, 1979), p. 150.
14. W. Backus and M. Chapian, *Telling Yourself the Truth* (Minneapolis: Bethany House Publishers, 1980), pp. 90, 101.
15. Dr Angelo Grazioli speaking at a Sexuality Today seminar at Waverley Abbey House, Farnham, July 1993.
16. J. Duin, op. cit., p. 69.

Chapter 3

1. Sara Tulloch (ed), *Reader's Digest Oxford Complete Wordfinder* (London: The Reader's Digest Association Ltd., 1993), p. 130.
2. J. Bowlby, *Attachment and Loss*, Volume 3: 'Loss, Sadness and Depression' (London: Penguin, 1981), p. 7.
3. Ibid., p. 27 (italics own).

4. D. Ross, *More Hugs* (New York: Crowell, 1984).
5. A. Atkins, *Split Image* (London: Hodder & Stoughton, 1987), pp. 206–207.
6. B. Ward, *Healing Grief* (London: Vermilion, 1993), p. 6.
7. J. Bowlby, op. cit., pp. 247–248.
8. B. Ward, op. cit., p. 123.
9. B. Ward, op. cit., p. 67.
10. Dr W. H. Frey II with Muriel Langseth, *Crying: The Mystery of Tears* (Minneapolis: Winston Press, 1985), p. 12.
11. G. Levoy, 'Tears That Speak', *Psychology Today* (August 1988), p. 8. Quoted in J. Smith and J. Biggs, *How to Say Goodbye* (Lynnwood: Aglow Publications, 1990).
12. J. Smith and J. Biggs, op. cit, pp. 19, 89.
13. Sarah Tulloch (ed), op. cit., pp. 1568, 1585.
14. J. Smith and J. Biggs, op. cit., p. 110.

Chapter 4

1. S. Page, *If I'm So Wonderful Why Am I Still Single?* (London: HarperCollins, 1993), p. 63.
2. H. I. Smith, *Singles Ask* (Minneapolis: Augsburg Publishing House, 1988), pp. 51–52. Number 1 taken from C. Cowan and M. Kinder, *Women Men Love, Women Men Leave* (New York: Clarkson N. Potter, 1987), pp. 21–26.
3. K. Keay, *Letters From A Solo Survivor* (London: Hodder & Stoughton, 1991), p. 97.
4. D. Mansell, 'The Single Person's Home – Pointless Stop-Gap or Pleasurable Meeting Point?', *Restoration Magazine* (November / December, 1988), p. 10.
5. L. McNeill Taylor, *Living Alone – A Woman's Guide* (London: Sheldon Press, 1987), p. 37.

Chapter 5

1. L. Harding, *Better Than Or Equal To?* (Milton Keynes: Pioneer / Word Books, 1993), p. 27.

2. S. Page, *If I'm So Wonderful Why Am I Still Single?* (London: HarperCollins, 1993), p. 30.

Chapter 6

1. W. E. Vine, *Expository Dictionary of Bible Words* (Basingstoke: Marshall, Morgan and Scott, 1978), p. 129.
2. A. Atkins, *Split Image* (London: Hodder & Stoughton, 1987), p. 51.
3. J. Duin, *Sex and the Single Christian* (London: Marshall Pickering, 1990).
4. John Littlewood, 'A Pastor's Perspective', *Singularly Significant News and Views*, no 1 (1993), p. 3.
5. A. Cornes, *Divorce and Remarriage* (London: Hodder & Stoughton, 1993), pp. 119, 125–126.
6. L. Harding, *Better Than Or Equal To?* (Milton Keynes: Pioneer / Word Books, 1993), pp. 90–91.

Chapter 7

1. C. Richard, *Single Minded* (London: Hodder & Stoughton, 1988), pp. 79–80.
2. F. D. Hammond, *Overcoming Rejection* (Chichester: Sovereign World, 1991), p. 68.
3. N. Cruz with M. Harris, *Lonely, But Never Alone* (Bristol: Don Summers Evangelistic Association, 1986), p. 156.
4. E. Fromm, *The Art of Loving* (London: Unwin Books, 1957), p. 38.
5. J. Duin, *Sex and the Single Christian* (London: Marshall Pickering, 1990), p. 38.
6. C. Richard, op. cit., p. 83.

Chapter 8

1. T. Horsfall, 'Ministering the Grace of God', *The Christian Counsellor*, Vol 1, no 3 (1991), p. 7.
2. 'Joyce Huggett Talking to Helena Wilkinson', *The Christian Counsellor*, vol 2, no 2 (1992), p. 3.

3. C. S. Lewis, *The Four Loves* (London: Collins Fount Paperbacks, 1977), p. 115.
4. Helena Wilkinson, Editorial *The Christian Counsellor*, vol 1, no 4 (1991), p. 1.
5. John Westfall, 'Starting Social for Singles', *Singularly Significant News and Views*, no 3 (1993), p. 2.

Chapter 9

1. G. Inrig, *Quality Friendship* (Chicago: Moody Press, 1981), p. 30.
2. Taken from Spiros Zodhiates (ed.) *Lexical Aid to the Old Testament in the Hebrew-Greek Key Study Bible: New American Standard Bible* (Chattanooga: AMG Publishers, 1990), p. 1726.
3. D. Johnson, *Reaching Out* (Englewood Cliffs: Prentice Hall, 1981), p. 5.
4. J. Conway, *Friendship* (Grand Rapids: Zondervan, 1989), p. 24.
5. G. Inrig, op.cit., p. 124.
6. A. Fernando, *Reclaiming Friendship* (Leicester: IVP, 1991), pp. 56–57.
7. B. Phillips, *The Delicate Art of Dancing with Porcupines* (Ventura: Regal Books, 1989).
8. A. Atkins, *Split Image* (London: Hodder & Stoughton, 1987), pp. 14, 24–25, 38.
9. G. Smalley with S. Scott, *For Better or For Best* (New York: Harper Paperbacks, 1979), pp. 26, 28–32.
10. J. Dobson, *Man to Man about Women* (Eastbourne: Kingsway, 1976), p. 15.
11. P. Tournier, *Marriage Difficulties* (London: SCM Press Ltd., 1967), pp. 16, 31, 34.
12. J. Dobson, op.cit., p. 27.
13. E. Fromm, *The Art of Loving* (London: Unwin Books, 1957), p. 32.
14. For more information read T. LaHaye, *Spirit Controlled Temperament* (Wheaton: Tyndale House Publishers, 1967).

15. *The Myers Briggs Type Indicator* (3803 East Bayshore Road, Palo Alto CA 94303, USA. Consulting Psychologists Press, Inc., 1988).

Chapter 10

1. C. G. Jung, *Modern Man in Search of a Soul* (London: Ark Paperbacks, 1984), p. 261.
2. J. Smith and J. Biggs, *How to Say Goodbye* (Lynnwood: Aglow Publications, 1990), p. 25.
3. M. Williams, *The Velveteen Rabbit*, miniature edition (London: William Heinemann Ltd., 1993), pp. 5–8.
4. For more information of this concept see J. White, *Changing on the Inside* (Guildford: Eagle, 1991).
5. E. Fromm, *The Art of Loving* (London: Unwin Books, 1957), pp. 9, 22–24.
6. J. Powell, SJ, *Fully Human, Fully Alive* (Niles: Argus Communications, 1976), pp. 20–22, 57.
7. Ibid., p. 23.
8. E. Elliot, *The Path of Loneliness* (Nashville: Thomas Nelson, 1988), p. 83.
9. Sara Tulloch (Ed), *Reader's Digest Oxford Complete Wordfinder* (London: The Reader's Digest Association Ltd., 1993), p. 649.
10. *Matthew Henry's Commentary* (Basingstoke: Marshall, Morgan and Scott, 1960), p. 635.
11. T. Horsfall, 'Ministering the Grace of God', *The Christian Counsellor*, vol 1, no 3 (1991), pp. 7–9.
12. E. Elliot, op. cit., p. 116.

Nicholaston House
Christian Retreat and Healing Centre

Helena Wilkinson is a part of the full-time, live-in team at Nicholaston House, on the Gower peninsula in South Wales. For further information on Helena's work and on the work of Nicholaston House visit the websites:

www.helenawilkinson.co.uk
www.nicholastonhouse.org

The vision for Nicholaston House came about long before it was purchased. Some thirteen years prior to the House coming on the market in 1998, a group of Christians in a Methodist Chapel in a rural location on Gower began praying for a place where people could get away from the stresses of life to receive help and rest. They believed that God would bring the centre into being and that their role was to pray for it. Meanwhile a couple in Surrey received a vision for 'a place where people who are hurting could come and find space'. A series of God-ordained events resulted in that couple, Derrick and Sue Hancock, moving to Swansea, becoming involved in Swansea City Mission, and the Mission purchasing Nicholaston House. Other people who now work at Nicholaston House had also had similar visions for a residential centre for healing, and hence the House is born out of the prayers, visions and longings of several people who, over the years, have had a heart to see God bring healing and restoration to broken lives.

In the entrance of the House are the words, 'In this place I will give peace'. People frequently comment on the peace they experience during their stay and the ways in which they encounter the presence of God in the House. As well as coming for rest, space and prayer ministry, people also come to Nicholaston House to participate in the week and weekend courses and retreats on offer. These events include prayer ministry, time out, creative activities, spiritual encouragement and insight, and support for those addressing a number of personal issues, such as eating disorders.

The location of the House itself is ideal for rest and renewal. Set in the heart of the Gower peninsula, an area of outstanding natural beauty, Nicholaston House overlooks the stunning Bay of Oxwich with its vast expanse of sand. In contrast, a country lane separates the back of the House from Cefn Bryn, where sheep, ponies, and cattle roam free across miles of open moorland. The whole area creates an ambiance of peace and tranquillity.

Inside the House, the downstairs comprises a sea-facing dining room, conservatory and lounge, a craft and bookstall, a purpose-built art and craft studio and two medium-sized conference rooms. The conference rooms can be opened up into one large room seating over 100 people.

Upstairs there is a lounge and a small chapel and library, as well as accommodation for around 28 people. All the bedrooms are en-suite (most are twin) and have colour television and tea- and coffee-making facilities. Many are sea-facing, and a passenger lift, as well as the main staircase, serve all. One bedroom is specifically adapted for those with disabilities – including wheelchair users. The disabled toilets, ramps and lift, make the House available to all.

The gardens, which overlook the sea, are designed to encourage relaxation and the House is a member of the

Quiet Gardens Trust.

If you would like to find out more about the work of Nicholaston House, then you can visit the website or write and ask for an information pack which includes details of the work, in-house events and resources.

Please send a large SAE to:

Nicholaston House, Penmaen, Gower,
Swansea SA3 2HL.
Tel: 01792 371317. Fax: 01792 371217.
Email: managers@nicholastonhouse.org